The Complete Book of
MOTORBOATING

The Complete Book of
MOTORBOATING

SELECTING, OUTFITTING, AND
MAINTAINING YOUR MOTORBOAT

BILL PIKE

SMITHMARK

A FRIEDMAN GROUP BOOK

This edition published in 1993 by SMITHMARK
Publishers, Inc., 16 East 32nd Street, New York,
NY 10016

ISBN 0-8317-0938-3

THE COMPLETE BOOK OF MOTORBOATING
Selecting, Outfitting, and Maintaining Your Motorboat
was prepared and produced by
Michael Friedman Publishing Group, Inc.
15 West 26th Street
New York, NY 10010

Editor: Elizabeth Viscott Sullivan
Art Director: Jeff Batzli
Designer: Ed Noriega
Photography Editor: Christopher C. Bain
Production: Jeanne E. Kaufman

Typeset by Classic Type, Inc.
Color separations by
United South Sea Graphic Art, Ltd.
Printed and bound in Hong Kong by
Leefung-Asco Printers Ltd.

SMITHMARK Books are available for bulk purchase
for sales promotion and premium use. For details
write or call the manager of special sales,
SMITHMARK Publishers Inc., 16 East 32nd Street,
New York, NY 10016; (212) 532-6600.

DEDICATION

To B.V.J.

TABLE OF CONTENTS

DON'T YOU EVER GET SICK OF BOATS?

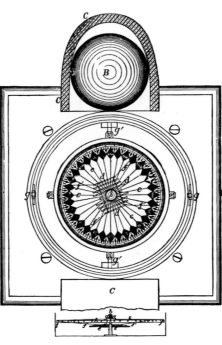

Although I have more than a nodding acquaintance with sailing vessels and more than a significant appreciation for them, I consider myself a motorboatman. By this, I mean a person who lives under the spell of the motorboat, a genre of waterborne conveyance that has enchanted people like me since the dawn of the engine.

As with all great passions, motorboating is part transcendent. It can transport the devotee to realms of experience and perception ineffably beyond the ordinary. It can make him feel utterly content, absolutely pleased with existence, even when he shouldn't be.

Some time ago, for a period of about five years, in the city marina of an offbeat, sun-baked Florida town called Gulfport, I cheerfully lived aboard a narrow, old fiberglass boat, *Misty,* where I slept among piles of sawdust and lived without air-conditioning, central heating, refrigeration, a telephone, a television, an automobile, or much of anything else, except power tools, which would qualify as a genuine twentieth-century convenience.

During those years, when I wasn't staying aboard *Misty* and slaving away on what I liked to call her "restoration," I was slaving away elsewhere, on ocean-going tugs, voyaging all over the world, or half of it, hitting one exotic port after another, a veritable addict for travel, adventure, and boats, especially of the mechanically propelled variety. For nearly half a decade, while living on one boat and working on several more, I never set foot inside a house. It was an idyllic sort of existence.

People who lead more normal lives have a hard time understanding the true motorboatman, primarily because they seem to have difficulty experiencing the transcendent aspects of motorboating. To them, the motorboat is simply another inanimate object. They find it difficult to understand how the relationship between motorboat and motorboatman can prosper under what appear to be adverse circumstances.

What a sweet vision: the tugboat. Tough and hardworking, with the economy of build and pugnacious style of a prizefighter, even small ones like Jupiter have a romance all their own.

One morning, toward the end of my "Gulfport Period," a marina friend was driving me over to Big Bend Power Plant on Tampa Bay, where, together with a fierce hangover and a big blue waterproof seabag full of damp, sawdust-tainted clothing, I was scheduled to board a mammoth tug, the *Betty Wood*, bound for Houston, Texas; Chile; Peru; Colombia; Mobile, Alabama; and finally back to Tampa, Florida.

People don't talk a lot while they're wailing through the countryside in a battered old Volkswagen bus at four o'clock in the morning. I don't think my friend said much of anything at all until we'd arrived at Big Bend. We were standing on the dock. It was time to shake hands and say so long.

"You know something, Pike?" he said, looking around, wryly observing the seeming chaos that envelops any big, oceangoing vessel just prior to her departure on an international voyage. In the orange glow of the mercury lights overhanging the dock, the frantic activities of crewmen and support people looked like writhing souls in hell.

"Sometimes I think you're absolutely crazy," he said. "Don't you ever get sick of boats?"

My motorboat enchantment began early, during the long, hot summer following my eleventh birthday, with the invention of a dog-powered, paddle wheel raft that sank shortly after launch. Luckily, my dog was an excellent swimmer and quick witted. He had little trouble extricating himself from the haphazard construct of waterlogged telephone poles I'd christened *Theseus*, in honor of a yarn my ex-schoolteacher grandmother had read me about the mythological adventures of an ancient Greek seafarer.

There was a mountain lake near the town I grew up in, and although my family moved from house to house quite often, we always kept our cottage on Wintergreen Bay, and our eighteen-foot (5.4-m) outboard-powered skiff. A friend of my father's owned a cottage across the lake from ours, where he kept a twenty-eight-foot (8.4-m) cabin cruiser, a creature of the Lone Star Boat Company, sheathed with great panels of aluminum riveted together, and painted dark green. There was a decorative shooting star emblazoned on the bow and room for twin Evinrudes at the transom.

One of the cruiser's most mysterious and enthralling facets was the small teak wheel mounted in the cockpit with which you steered the boat. Before then, I'd seen such things in movies only. The cruiser had a cabin, accessed via a varnished plywood door in the bulkhead at the forward edge of the cockpit. The cabin held bunks, which hinted strongly at circumnavigations of the lake, perhaps the world.

I remember my first tour of that twenty-eight-foot (8.4-m) boat taken while she nodded dockside like a spirited pony. As my father and I jumped aboard, her outboard motors, still warm from a run, filled the soft summer evening with the exotic scent of gasoline mixed with oil. It was as heady a perfume as any I've smelled since. To this day, the smell of a small, two-cycle outboard raises my hackles and sets me dreaming of voyages to enigmatic places.

While the men talked, I sat on one of the bunks inside, listening to the lake lap against the hull. The sun was setting outside the Plexiglas windows, yet enveloped the boxy little cabin with the red glow of a magic lamp. I remember well the feeling I had at that moment, a mixture of peacefulness and expectation. And I've had that same feeling many times since, aboard one motorboat or another.

There are many types of modern motorboats, and many types of motorboat-men. In the following pages, we're going to take a look at both. We'll also have some fun with the history of motorboating. We'll examine the modern marine engine and how it developed. We'll discuss how to buy a motorboat and how to properly outfit yourself and your vessel to get the most out of your voyaging. We'll look at the essentials of motorboating safety and, finally, at just a few of the ways you can have fun with motorboats.

While reading this book, you'll come across a sea story or two, excerpted either from my years of commercial seafaring or from the often concomitant years of messing about in recreational motorboats. I include these stories in the hope that they may brighten up the rare dull spots in an otherwise fascinating sport.

The moods of motorboating are many. Stand alone on the bridge of a towering sportfisherman (center) and feel the civilized world disappear astern. Or walk a tired old beach (above) and dream.

CHAPTER ONE

A BRIEF HISTORY OF MOTORBOATING

What is motorboating? Many forms of activity qualify as long as they involve the movement of a vehicle through the water by means of some sort of propulsive device (i.e. motor)—the pleasant result being that less sweat and bother are expended on the enterprise than otherwise might be.

While the concept of motorboating is perhaps older than one might suspect, it evolved out of an even older and more fundamental idea—the boat. Somewhere, long before recorded history began, somebody, somewhere, imagined being able to float upon the water in one way or another. And then that inventive somebody decided to put his vision to the test.

Let's take a brief look at the development of the boat and then examine in some detail the various advances in the realms of design and propulsion that have made the modern motorboat what it is today.

BOATS AND OARS

The oldest ancestor of the boat was probably a simple log. Since joining a couple of logs together with some vines and creepers was not exactly taxing, even to a Neanderthal intelligence, it's reasonable to assume that the next development, the raft, came pretty quickly.

It was then discovered that the use of an odd number of logs made things go more smoothly. A pointed and therefore more hydrodynamic configuration could be obtained by simply flanking a longer center log with some shorter ones. Thus was invented the first bow of a watercraft.

The Egyptians should be given credit for building the first real boat. Although some historians maintain that the Egyptians were handicapped by a lack of wood, they actually had plenty, at least during the early period of their boat building, several thousand years B.C. At the time, Egypt was a lot less sandy than it is today, with forests of acacia, sycamore, and persea.

Getting there is half the fun, but sometimes it can be a little complicated. From the rowboats of the ancients to tricyclelike contraptions with humongous pneumatic wheels, the history of motorboating has its eccentricities.

Besides raw material, the Egyptians had a great deal of incentive. Their rafts, for which they were duly famous, tended to sink with inordinate alacrity, primarily because the papyrus with which they were made absorbs water. With luck, large rafts might have lasted a year or two, and small ones only a couple of months.

An interim solution to this problem was the dugout canoe. Years before the first Egyptian riverboat was built, the ancients discovered that by hollowing out a log, they could create a vehicle that was lighter and much faster than a raft. They also discovered that dugouts were drier and easier to steer than log rafts, yet had about the same buoyancy. This was fine, except that dugouts were difficult to build.

There had to be an easier way. About 4000 B.C., a savvy but now-forgotten Egyptian genius had a brainstorm. Why not build something like a dugout, but use light, easy-to-manage pieces instead of wasting time digging all that clunky old wood out of a log with a stone scraper? So, the first full-fledged boat had an eye-shaped flat bottom and two long, rectangular sides. Despite the fact that the boat was made of three pieces, it had an assured, together look. (Because everyone was in such a hurry to try the weird little conveyance out, there was no time to invent fasteners like nails or screws. The boat was sewn together with the ancient equivalent of today's rawhide.)

No one knows exactly how the seams of these early boats were caulked to prevent leaks. After a time, larger vessels were created, some of them more than eighty feet (24 m) long, by sewing on extra planks. As boats became more complex, the use of wooden pegs to hold them together became necessary.

Oars were a later invention. It was around 3000 B.C. when the Egyptians discovered that their boats could be propelled up the Nile, against the current with sticks. When these sticks were not long enough to touch bottom, they could be used to scull the vessels along, meaning that these rudimentary oars, employed at the sterns of the boats, were moved from side to side and turned obliquely at the end of each stroke so as to administer thrust.

At heart, King Tut was probably a motorboating type, although ancient Egyptian vessels like this one were quite unsophisticated. Why else would the Egyptians have invented oars?

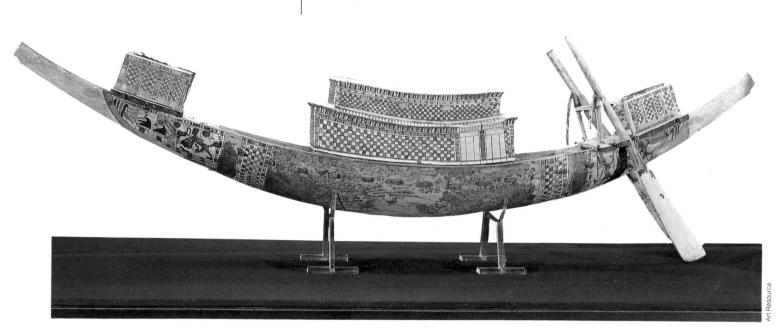

From the sculling technique, the invention of oars as we know them today required a short but brilliant burst of creativity. Eventually, the Egyptians would travel the ancient world prodigiously in long, slim vessels propelled by oars— the harbingers of the motorboating mentality. Here at last were boats and boatmen with propulsion systems that could take them virtually anywhere, regardless of current or wind. No more hanging around, thumbs a-twiddle, praying for favorable sailing conditions.

The name of the inventor of the oar is as forgotten as the name of the inventor of the boat. Nevertheless, the person's influence was prodigious. Bas-reliefs on Egyptian monuments dating from as early as 2000 B.C. depict vessels equipped with as many as forty oarsmen. It is a known fact that these boats regularly traveled back and forth between Crete and the mouth of the Nile. In time, other peoples, including the Phoenicians, Greeks, Romans, and Vikings, would all build boats that were propelled by oars.

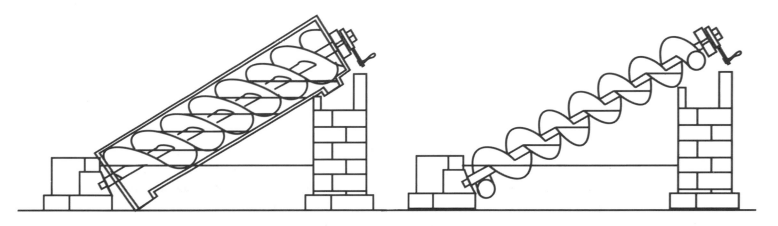

STREAKING AND OTHER GREEK FEATS

With the ascendancy of Alexander the Great, Egypt built a marvelous city, Alexandria, and a magnificent library there that became the stomping grounds of one of the most famous scientists of all time: Archimedes, the father of marine propulsion.

According to historians, Archimedes came from Syracuse, on the east coast of Sicily, and rose to prominence about the third century B.C. Although the rotary screw-type machine he invented then was initially applied in the field of agriculture as an irrigation pump, the theory would serve later inventors in the marine field well.

"Archimedes' screw" (or an Archimedean screw) was basically a cylinder with a continuous spiral or screw within. Turn the cylinder with one end immersed in an irrigation ditch, and water could be raised via the screw within and expelled at the other end. Turn the cylinder the other way, and thrust was generated, although no one was interested in this aspect at the time. No one was interested either in the fact that an increase in the cylinder's speed of rotation caused an increase in thrust.

Would you believe that the modern screw propeller got its start in an irrigation ditch? There are several versions of Archimedes' screw, two of which appear above. Crank the handle one way and water is lifted to a higher level; crank the handle the other way and you've got the rudiments of propulsion.

Archimedes was a heavy thinker, and he invented important motorboating concepts such as displacement. Although he appears fully clothed here, he did some of his best thinking when he was naked as a jaybird in the bathtub.

Archimedes made more than one contribution to marine science and thus motorboating. He also discovered what he called his "First Principle," an idea that has figured one way or another in the construction of every motorboat that was built since that time. The First Principle simply states that a solid body (such as the hull of a motorboat) immersed in a liquid (such as water) is buoyed up by a force equal to the weight of the liquid it displaces. Today, the weight of a motorboat is called its "displacement," and the term and what it represents is an integral part of the calculations that are part and parcel of boat design.

The story of how Archimedes hit upon his First Principle starts out humbly enough, somewhere around 200 B.C. in Syracuse.

King Hiero, a local politician with plenty of clout, decided he needed a new crown, and let out bids to that effect. Since there weren't that many crown companies around in those days, there were only two applicants for the job. The two parties built their crowns and submitted them for the king's inspection. Hiero picked a winner. Money was about to change hands when the loser started complaining. He said the gold in the low bidder's crown had been adulterated with silver to cut costs.

Nobody, least of all the king, could tell whether the complaint was justified or not. Both crowns looked practically identical. Hiero called for the chief scientist, Archimedes, to solve the problem.

The solution came to Archimedes while he was taking a bath; he observed that when he lowered himself into a full tub, water spilled over the sides. Wouldn't a crown made of a combination of gold and a lighter, cheaper metal like silver, be bulkier than one made of pure gold? And wouldn't the bulkier crown spill more water?

Archimedes was so excited by his theorizing that he made an ungarbed dash to his laboratory, where, still naked as a jaybird, he began to test his ideas. First, Archimedes measured out a mass of pure gold equal to the weight of the suspect crown. He then immersed both the mass and the crown in two identical containers of water and measured the overflows. He discovered that the volume of water displaced by the suspect crown was greater than that displaced by the chunk of gold. "Eureka," cried Archimedes. The suspect crown was indeed a fraud. Thus the First Principle and "streaking," a form of naked exhibitionism that showed a marked resurgence in popularity in the 1970s, were born.

MOTORBOATING WITH THE ROMANS

Although the use of oars was invented by the Egyptians and further developed and refined by the Phoenicians and the Greeks, it was the Romans who, with characteristic practicality, improved upon and then surpassed the technique.

Reaching a state of perfection during the second century A.D., the Roman trireme was one of the most efficient oar-propelled vessels of all time, bar none. Triremes were as large as 140 feet (42 m) long and contained three full tiers of oars on each side, pulled by synchronized teams of galley slaves.

Marine engineers say that the basic, no-frills trireme, loaded with a full complement of slaves, was capable of moving through the water at about six knots. The engineers hasten to add that their calculations may be off by as much as 50 percent. Thus, the average trireme may have been capable of speeds in the neighborhood of nine or ten knots.

Six knots is incredible. Ten's not much slower than the speed at which a modern vessel of roughly comparable size would run, with a pair of locomotive engines in her belly.

No nation of seafarers, before or since, has manufactured such mind-boggling power from human sweat and blood. Most triremes were double ended, meaning that both the forward and after portions of the craft were pointed. Rudders, for steering, also were mounted fore and aft, so enemy vessels were never sure whether the trireme was coming or going. Slaves sat cater-cornered to the center of the boat, looking forward and slightly outboard. They didn't so much row as scull along, Egyptianlike, generating thrust on both the inboard and outboard strokes, without ever actually lifting their oars from the water.

By A.D. 300, Roman triremes, and smaller biremes (with two instead of three tiers of slaves), had cleared the Mediterranean of pirates. Besides progress in the realm of propulsion, the development of these vessels represented great advances in the field of displacement-hull construction. No longer were boats built of planks and sewn together. Instead, an interior structure of hardwood ribs was covered with strips of wood and fastened mechanically, producing hulls that were sleek, smooth, and fast. With considerable refinement, this method of construction would persist among boatbuilders well into the future, until the development of fiberglass toward the middle of the twentieth century.

In A.D. 527, a wild idea percolated up from the collective unconscious—mechanical propulsion. Heretofore, Roman boatmen were basically content to go fast and carry a big whip. But the prospect of a more efficient propulsion system than the oar-slave combination prompted an anonymous Roman inventor to mount twin paddle wheels on a galley. Whether this worked well or not is hard to say. But the idea was good. Paddle wheels are more sophisticated than oars. And they're certainly more adaptable to machinery, even of the most rudimentary nature.

A bas-relief from the time of Claudius Caudex shows a Roman cruiser with three paddle wheels on each side, driven by three pairs of oxen. The machinery? Either the beasts turned a big capstan, which in turn moved the wheels through a system of gears, or they hoofed it along treadmills. One way or the other, seasickness and broken legs undoubtedly took their toll.

THE RENAISSANCE CONTRIBUTION

Born in 1452, the natural son of a Florentine notary and a peasant girl, Leonardo da Vinci exemplified Renaissance genius. One of his inventions, the bilge pump, is still popular today, especially aboard sinking watercraft.

But bilge pumps were really small potatoes. Hull shapes were Leonardo's forte. Until he began experimenting with them, boat bottoms were either round or flat, or a combination of both. Their stability, meaning the ability to resist tipping over, was not good. To improve stability, Leonardo came up with the first V-bottom hull. Based on his extensive studies of fish, he gave it a distinctly piscine shape when looked at in cross section. Besides improving stability, Leonardo predicted that the V-shaped bottom would improve speed and handling by reducing water resistance. He was right. The majority of motorboats today have V-shaped bottoms of one type or another.

Weird science is not a totally modern thing. The oddball, oxen-activated propulsion system (opposite page) is almost as strange as this monstrosity invented by Leonardo da Vinci (left), and an early version of the modern screw propeller (below). Can you figure out John Fitch's direct propulsion scheme (bottom) that was developed in the early 1790s?

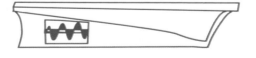

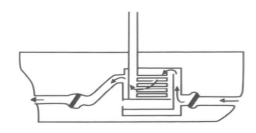

THE MODERN SCREW PROPELLER

About the mid-eighteenth century, an urge to go motorboating that had been smoldering, almost forgotten since the onset of the Renaissance, burst into flames. Sailboats continued to dominate the marine scene, of course, as they had for hundreds of years. But the age of the machine was at hand, the Industrial Revolution. There simply had to be a way to build boats powered exclusively by machine. In 1729, Dr. John Allen patented a jet-propelled boat in England, rejecting paddle wheels and oars entirely.

Originally, Allen's plans had called for a crew to operate a pump, which would discharge air from the stern at five-second intervals. Obviously, speed depended on the esprit de corps of the crew. To reduce the uncertainty associated with the human element, Allen struck upon an interesting alternative, one that, in a way, heralded the invention of the internal-combustion engine about a century hence.

He suggested that a stout chamber be built at the stern of his boat. The chamber was to be so configured that gunpowder explosions inside would drive the boat ahead. Understandably, Allen had a tough time hiring people to man his vessels, and an even tougher time recruiting passengers.

The Swiss got in on the action in 1759, when a cleric by the name of Monseigneur Genevois was inspired to concoct a boat that was driven by mechanical oars resembling the feet of aquatic birds. The energy to move these feet was stored in giant springs. Later, in 1787, on the Delaware River, John Fitch operated the first successful mechanically propelled steamboat, a full twenty years before Robert Fulton's paddle-wheel-powered *Clermont* made its famous trip up the Hudson River, terrifying scads of lubberly cows and farmers in the process.

By the early part of the nineteenth century, just about every propulsion device familiarly used by modern motorboatmen, and many devices not so familiarly used, had either been suggested or tested. Not only had inventors given jet propulsion, air, and water screws a good try, they had also experimented with mechanical duck and goose feet, provocatively thrusting umbrellalike cones, vibrating boards, as well as wind-driven, ox-driven, and man-powered paddle wheels…all in the name of motorboating.

There was one device, however, that had yet to be perfected—the screw propeller. Since Archimedes, people had been experimenting with screw-like propulsion devices, but nothing seemed to work in a practical, everyday sort of way.

Then, in 1808, an English grazing farmer, Francis Petit Smith, and a Swedish gentleman, John Ericsson, each simultaneously created screw propellers that closely resembled the ones that push most motorboats through the water today. Modern screw propellers are often called "wheels" and are usually comprised of from two to five blades or "buckets" emanating from a central hub, which turns on a shaft via an engine. Screw propellers are named as such because of the twist in each of the blades. If one were somehow turned in a solid material, such as a piece of wood, it would carve out a spiral much as a wood screw does. The modern propeller, with its separate blades, is much more efficient than an Archimedean screw, which is essentially a single, spiral plate wrapped around a central cone.

Despite the best efforts of both Petit Smith and Ericsson, the screw propeller was not an immediate success, at least in small craft. At the time, there were no engines powerful enough to turn small propellers fast enough to produce real thrust. Steam engines had the power to turn big propellers on ships, but they were too heavy for small boats.

Internal-combustion engines changed all this. Sure, the earliest models were heavy and hydrogen powered. But eventually, during the latter part of the nineteenth century, they became light enough and powerful enough to be practical in small watercraft. When these gasoline-powered "stink pots" came into their own, so did the screw propeller.

Another early version of the modern screw propeller.

REVEREND RAMUS'S PLANING HULL

Although people had been watching flat stones skip efficiently across ponds for thousands of years, it wasn't until 1872 that anybody thought to apply this principle to motorboats.

The inventor of the planing hull was an Englishman, Reverend C. M. Ramus, of Rye, in Sussex. He built a boat with a flat-bottomed hull and an upturned bow that could glide or skip across the waves, rather than plow through them.

Ramus also had the idea of creating a "stepped hull," which had two planing surfaces: one deeper in the water and forward, the other higher and near the stern. As it moved across the water, the stepped hull would ride on the two surfaces and be buoyed up by the air and turbulence trapped at the "step" between them.

Ramus was considered a crackpot by his contemporaries. His model ships refused to plane, mostly because they were too heavy and too big. Ships, even today, don't plane.

But if anyone, Ramus included, had thought to try his planing theories on small boats, the ungainly looking stepped hydroplane, which brought the wild excitement of speed to the twentieth century, would have appeared upon the motorboating scene much earlier than it actually did.

Below are drawings of Reverend Ramus's hydroplane. Figure 6 shows a three-point planing shape, the precursor of today's three-point hydroplanes.

Figure 1

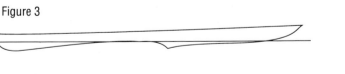

Figure 2

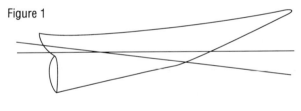

Figure 3

Figure 4

Figure 5

Figure 6

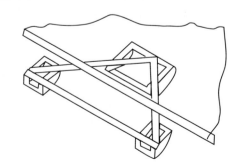

SPEEEEEEED!

Among the burgeoning group of people who called themselves motorboatmen, speed was not too terribly important until the 1920s.

Then, fast and flashy racing boats, with planing hulls, stepped bottoms, and big, high-horsepower internal-combustion engines, drew vast crowds of spectators to the shores of the Saint Lawrence and the Detroit rivers in America, the Seine in France, and the Thames in England, anywhere where there was a lot of open, relatively flat water.

Never have there been, before or since, motorboats quite like the typical Gold Cup racers of the Jazz Age. Made of varnished mahogany, with pianolike satin finishes, Gold Cup boats were half dragster, half limousine.

They bore names like *Baby Bootlegger*, *Hotsy-Totsy*, and *Rowdy*; their machinery spaces chockablock with fighter plane engines, these boats went wailing across the water at speeds scoffed at only a few decades before. Whoooooooeeeee—the speedboat had arrived.

Gold Cup racers likc Dixie II were some of the most beautiful speedboats to ever grace a waterway. Generally made of varnished mahogany and burnished to the sheen of grand pianos, they were sometimes powered with fighter plane engines.

THE LAST WORD... PLASTIC

With World War II came the last motorboating development we're going to talk about. It began with the discovery of glues that were impervious to water, and the rediscovery of some of the strangest cloth anybody had ever laid eyes on.

As the war continued in Europe, a few innovative and enterprising souls in the United States began playing around with a new method of boat building that blended three essentials that had never been combined before: (1) water-resistant resin, (2) a cavity mold, and (3) fiberglass cloth, a highly unusual material, woven from fibers of glass, first invented by the French in the nineteenth century.

The first fiberglass boats were built using molds that were more complex than the ones used today. Resin technology was not very advanced in its beginnings, and hulls were often difficult to dry thoroughly, or "cure," which meant molds had to be built that could accommodate pipes for steam or some other means for drying the laminate inside.

Today, fiberglass boat building is simpler. Briefly, here's how it's done. First, a builder carefully makes a "plug" or mock-up of the boat he wants to build, using wood, putty, fairing compound, and whatever else is necessary. He covers the plug with fiberglass cloth, using brushes and other tools to "wet it out," or saturate it with liquid resin. This laminating process is repeated several times; each layer of laminate is allowed to dry between applications. When the entire fiberglass construct covering the plug is cured, the builder pulls it off very carefully. Now he has a cavitylike mold that can be used to build a number of boats that will duplicate the shape of the plug. The actual construction of a vessel is much like the construction of the mold. The builder simply creates another laminate, applying cloth and resin, in stages, to the inner surface of the cavity mold.

The development of fiberglass sparked a veritable motorboating boom during the 1950s and early 1960s, the effects of which we are still experiencing today. Boat builders went wild, forsaking molded plywood—which had only recently become popular—for the advantages of plastic. Why not? They could create vessels of every conceivable shape and size. And fiberglass boats were easy to build, strong, rot resistant, and comparatively cheap to buy and maintain.

Today, one of the main attributes of the motorboat is the variety with which it manifests. Pick up any marine magazine on the newsstand and peruse a page or two. You'll discover that there are all kinds of motorboats on the market, and on the water. The five or six major categories, in fact, are the subject of our next chapter.

Building the modern fiberglass boat has become almost as much of an art form as building boats of wood used to be. Manufacturing facilities are generally clean and efficiently organized, like the one pictured here. The future of boat building? Some boat companies are working to develop alternative building processes beyond fiberglass; they're using new plastics that can be recycled.

CHAPTER TWO

I ALWAYS WANTED A DARN TRAWLER

Walk the docks of serious watering holes in places as diverse as Fort Lauderdale, Florida, and Portofino, Italy, and you'll see vessels tied alongside that dwarf everything else in the neighborhood. Called megayachts, these things are usually blindingly white, with varnished teak accents and amenities such as waterfalls in the johns and stand-up Jacuzzis in the wheelhouses. Such boats sell for millions, and they occupy one end of the motorboat spectrum.

At the other extreme are the cheapies. Called skiffs, john boats, and pirouges, you'll find them holding up the walls of mercantile establishments in just about every town, village, and city in the world. Anywhere from eight to eighteen feet (2 to 5.4 m) long, made of plywood, fiberglass, or aluminum, flat-, round-, or V-bottomed and low sided, they fill motorboating's bargain basement.

Literally thousands upon thousands of motorboats of every possible size and shape are encompassed between these two extremes. For simplicity's sake, we'll break them up into approximately six categories, although, technically speaking, there are even more.

The modern cruising trawler is probably the saltiest, most romantic-looking motorboat plying the briny today.

ALL ABOUT RUNABOUTS

If there's a symbol of motorboating democracy, it's the runabout. Almost every motorboatman has owned one at one time during his life. If you're new to the sport and a little mystified by it all, a runabout might well be your best initial purchase. The runabout is the least complicated motorboat to own and maintain—but let's qualify that statement. There are simpler motor-propelled watercraft, but dinghies, skiffs, and the like are a bit too small to consider here.

Basically, runabouts are small, planing-type boats. This means that, at speed, their hulls tend to ride over the surface of the water, like a skipping stone, rather than through it. Slow a planing runabout down and it soon settles back into the water and begins pushing a wave at the bow. (To my knowledge, there are no true displacement-type runabouts. Displacement craft are more fuel efficient than planing boats as a rule, but they're also much slower. Given its name, a displacement runabout would constitute a contradiction in terms. For more on displacement, see chapter 1.)

Runabouts usually measure less than twenty-six feet (7.8 m) from stem to stern, and contain one cockpit, although it used to be the fashion to have two or more cockpits. As the name bowrider implies, some runabouts have seating in the bow.

Runabouts are usually open boats, but often sport bimini tops as protection from the elements. They may have either one or two engines. Today, most installations involve a type of engine drive-train package called a stern drive (see chapter 3). The rest, primarily water-ski boats and "gentleman's runabouts" are inboards, that is, the engine is inside the boat and the propellers turn via shafts through the boat's bottom.

Runabout hull shapes vary. The cathedral, or gull-wing, type became quite popular during the 1970s, but has since become scarce, although Boston Whaler and a few other manufacturers have stuck with the design, to the advantage of scads of motorboatmen. The cathedral hull is like three hulls in one. A V-shaped center section is flanked by two sponsons at the chines (or sides) of the hull, with cathedral-like arches in between. The sponsons tend to stabilize the craft, both at rest and when under way, so it is less tippy. The downside is the ride. Cathedral hulls tend to pound in a chop, slamming their bows against the surface of the water at planing speed.

A second type is the modified-V hull; the majority of modern runabouts have modified-Vs. This means that, when viewed from just ahead, the bow has a distinct, V-like shape. In a modified-V hull, the sharpness of this V diminishes throughout the length of the boat, until at the stern the angle measured between a horizontal line and a leg of the V (dead rise) will be about eighteen or twenty degrees. The modified-V seems to work best for most runabout boats today. The sharp, forward end of the boat cuts the water and obviates the tendency to pound inherent in more curved surfaces. The flatter, after portion of the boat lends stability to the ride.

Modern replicas of old mahogany runabouts, or restorations of them, give the sport of motorboating a time-machinelike ambiance.

Although they're not particularly prevalent in runabouts, the best heavy-weather hulls are deep-Vs. Deadrise at the transom of a deep-V is about twenty-six degrees, not much less, and continues forward unchanged. The bow cuts the seas like a knife, as does the rest of the bottom. However, there are some drawbacks to a deep-V. More horsepower is required to get one on plane. Also, a deep-V doesn't turn quite as easily as a modified-V because of its hull's lateral resistance to movement.

Another quirk with deep-Vs is stability. While underway, deep-Vs may tend to rock from side to side or "chine-walk," or, particularly in a crosswind, lay over slightly on one side and try to run that way. Such tendencies can be corrected by using devices known as trim tabs. Trim tabs are located in pairs at the transom of a boat. They can be adjusted like the flaps of an airplane to alter the boat's running attitude.

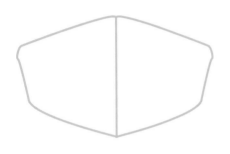

There are all kinds of motorboat hulls. The flat-bottom hull (top) is one of the simplest and most common hulls. The round-bottom hull (bottom) is fairly common, too. The deep-V hull (opposite page, top) is most prominent in offshore raceboats, and the cathedral hull (opposite page, bottom) seems to be dying out.

Static stability, or stability at rest, can be a problem, too. This is not to say that a deep-V is going to tip over at the dock. It simply means that, while having a great deal of initial or reserve stability, it can quite easily tip a little bit.

Again, there are a few deep-V runabouts on the market. The genre is most highly represented in racing and sport boats.

So what defines a runabout? First, its small size. Second, its easy maneuverability, which makes it an ideal teacher for a prospective motorboatman who wants to learn boathandling. Runabouts are also less affected by wind and current, which also makes things less complicated for the novice. Moreover, they are usually cheaper to own and maintain than most larger vessels, so unless you hit something expensive with your runabout, like a megayacht, operating costs may be kept to a minimum.

There is one exception to the rule about lower cost. Patrician rather than democratic, the modern gentleman's runabout is built to resemble any of several elegant old-time pleasure boats, like the Gold Cup racers of the 1920s. In deference to the busy lives of today's wealthy owners, it is often constructed in such a way as to eliminate the maintenance headaches associated with its ancestors.

Some gentleman's runabouts are made entirely of fiberglass, like most other mainstream runabouts, but get the old-fashioned look from solid chrome-plated castings and fitments that lend an aura of antiquity to their subtly high-tech decks. One company has even patented a process whereby its fiberglass hulls are made to look like mahogany.

Chris Craft's remake of their old 1930 mahogany runabout adds another twist. Beneath a traditional-looking cosmetic layer of Honduras mahogany, with seven coats of varnish, the actual construction of the boat is quite modern, although it does involve sawed frames, conventional fastenings, and longitudinal battens throughout, just like the original. The modernity? W.E.S.T. system epoxy is used to impregnate the structural mahogany. Wooden boats built like this are at least as strong as fiberglass, and seem to have all of its advantages. They are impervious to rot and their seams will not open and

leak when the boat is removed from the water, as the seams on regular wooden boats will.

I had a chance to drive a Chris Craft remake one October afternoon, and it was an experience. Taking a ride in a runabout like this would ultimately sell even the lubberliest person on motorboating. There were two other people in the boat with me, one of them being Christopher Columbus Smith, the grandson of the founder of Chris Craft. We sped across the autumnal Long Island chop, veritable kings of the road. The stainless steel cutwater at the bow sliced the froth, and we were all smiling, ensconced in an elegant time machine.

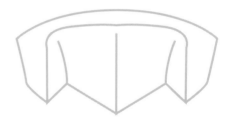

As noted earlier, except for pricey antiques or pseudo antiques like the Chris, the runabout is the easiest motorboat to own, from a financial standpoint. The best way to get an idea of how much runabouts cost is to read the boating magazines, particularly those that are devoted to boats under twenty-six feet (7.8 m).

What do you use a runabout for? Day trips, mostly. If the beaches are sandy you can often run the runabout ashore, jump off, and go exploring or picnicking. But the real excitement comes from driving the wild blue yonder, feeling the wind in your hair, the fresh air and sun on your face, and the exhilarating brand of freedom only a small motorboat can give.

ODE TO A TRAWLER

I guess every motorboatman has his favorite type of motorboat, and the trawler is mine. More closely than any other type, the trawler resembles actual working boats, which are near and dear to my heart. I'd like to say that a healthy concern for our dwindling energy reserves plays a part in my love affair with trawlers: they probably burn less fuel per pound of displacement than any other motorboat type. Actually, the truth is that part of my reason for liking trawlers is wallet centered. I don't like spending a lot of money at the pump.

The reason for the trawler's efficiency is its hull shape. Where most runabouts are built flat, to plane or skim the surface of the water, the displacement hull of the trawler has a rounder bottom and a sharp bow, enabling it to slip efficiently through the water. Some trawlers have soft chines or no chines at all. Hull sides and bottom don't meet at an angle but blend together in a curve; some hulls have bottoms that are almost semicircular in cross section.

Trawlers don't need to be lightweight since they're not built to plane. They're built broad, or "beamy," so they can be filled with stores and cruising paraphernalia. Besides all the comforts of home, the interiors of trawlers, especially those built in Taiwan, are famous for their fancy woodwork. Walls and bulkheads are often planked with teak or mahogany, and decks are usually covered with parquets of the same material.

If you've decided to sell the house, turn sea dog and live aboard, you're probably going to be looking at some trawlers. If you buy one, you're going to make a host of pleasant discoveries, not the least of them being the trawler's gift for comfort. There's probably no better way to spend an evening than in the salon of an Albin or Grand Banks, stretched out on a settee, reading a book

The true fishing trawler, from which the recreational trawler evolved, has a full-displacement hull. True trawlers have deep-draft, hefty hulls that are much more seaworthy than their cruising cousins.

about the vicissitudes of rounding Cape Horn while the boat swings peacefully at anchor in some comfortable cove.

Because of their hull shape, trawlers have a certain notoriety. They roll. If you're prone to seasickness, or think you may be, forego trawler trips, especially in beam seas.

Don't misunderstand. A trawler is as seaworthy as any other type of boat. Probably more so in some situations. Sea conditions that would send runabouts and some small cruisers packing will often not deter a trawler, which simply slows down and keeps plugging along—and rolling nauseatingly.

Why do trawlers roll? It's not complicated. Most pleasure boats, including trawlers, have the least amount of draft possible. Two reasons for this are: (1) less hull in the water means less water resistance and consequently more speed, and (2) some scenic spots are shallow, no pun intended. A trawler's lack of draft makes it more versatile, capable of shallow-water poking around or "gunkholing."

But here's the rub. Coupled with lofty superstructures reminiscent of deep-draft commercial fishing boats, the trawler's lack of draft produces top-heaviness that, in turn, produces a sickening roll. To counteract this, trawlers are often outfitted with hydraulic stabilizers, mechanical fins that protrude from the hull and move automatically to reduce roll.

Another way to take the roll out of a trawler, at least at anchor, is to use "flopper-stoppers," circular frames covered with heavy wire mesh and flaps of rubber. These are deployed in pairs on outriggers, one on either side of the boat; they sink readily, but are quite obstinate about returning to the surface when the flaps seal off against the mesh on the bottom. Flopper-stoppers don't

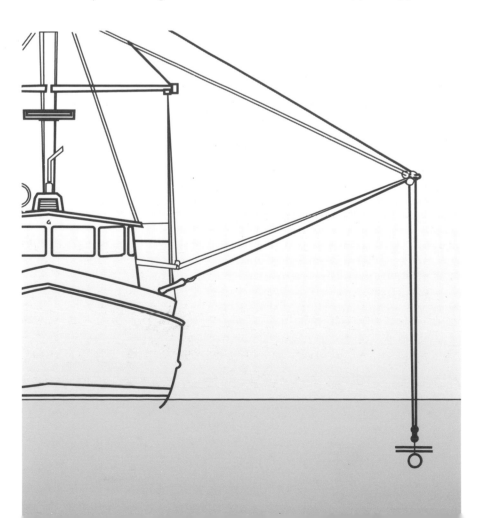

"Flopper-stoppers,"
sometimes called paravanes,
tend to stabilize trawlers
with round-bottom
displacement hulls and keep
them from rocking back and
forth when underway.
Deployed on either side
of the vessel, "flopper-
stoppers" are trolled like
giant fishing lures.

Civilian performance boats are fast, but still provide many amenities, including everything from berths for sleeping to ice makers and sun pads.

© Allan Weitz

stop roll, but do reduce it. Also, paravanes, winged metal devices that are trolled on booms like giant fishing lures, will stabilize a trawler under way, perhaps doing a better job of it than hydraulic stabilizers.

Two other trawler idiosyncracies are cost and handling. Top-of-the-line trawlers are expensive. The reason for this is that they're built to live aboard for short or extended periods of time. Thus, they contain many extras: generators for electricity when at anchor, refrigerators, microwave ovens, king-size beds, galleys with double sinks, and so on.

Handling a trawler can be tough. Many of them have single engines, for the sake of increased fuel efficiency. Most people will tell you that a boat with a single engine is more difficult to maneuver than one with twins.

The best way to learn how to handle a trawler is to get some old salt to teach you. Failing that, remember one thing. To get the most out of a single-screw vessel, you've got to make both the peculiarities of the boat and the vagaries of nature work for you. Try to fool with either one and you may wind up in a docking situation where the spectators are later called upon as witnesses.

Some malcontents would argue that the single-screw advantages of a trawler do not outweigh the handling disadvantages. Because there is no opposite torque produced in a counter-rotating mate, a single-screw boat tends to have a maneuvering bias.

A bias is rarely a problem when running ahead, since its effects are minor. However, boats move astern much slower than they do ahead. Per given revolution, any propeller has much more pushing than pulling power. When a trawler backs down, the bias is much more noticeable because of the inefficiencies involved, and the stern tends to swing one way or the other, depending upon the direction of rotation of the propeller.

LANDINGS, PORT AND STARBOARD

When going astern, a trawler with a propeller with right-hand rotation will back to port, meaning, to the left. This can be used to advantage by skippers who have the foresight to arrange their landings portside to. It's simple. With the engine running slowly ahead and the steering mechanism or rudder to starboard, meaning, to the right, you nose the bow slowly up to the dock at an angle of about twenty degrees, shifting the engine to neutral as soon as possible to reduce speed. Then, when you're close to where you want to be, you shift your engine from neutral to astern. This slows your progress and kicks the stern sweetly into the dock.

Starboard-side landings require the use of a technique that requires more finesse. To tie up this way, you simply nose up to the dock again, same angle, different side, making sure that you're running dead slow; slower, say, than you would be if you were docking on the portside. As you get close to where you want to be, shift your rudder over to the left so that it angles away from the dock. Coasting in, shift the engine out of neutral and give it a shot of forward thrust, just enough to swing the stern to starboard. Then, to stop your forward motion, shift astern for a quick shot, and then back to neutral. The initial burst forward kicks the stern into the dock, and the reverse thrust astern counteracts it, stopping your trawler where you want it—right in front of Harry's Clam Bar.

DEMONS OF SPEED

A high-performance boat is one that goes like a bat out of hell. I've driven a bunch of them in my capacity as a boating writer, and I always look forward to driving a new one. If you ask race boat drivers, the men and women who ram around the high seas in the neighborhood of a hundred miles (160 km) per hour for hours on end, they'll tell you that going superfast on the water is like a drug. You can get hooked.

High-performance boats can be broken down into two categories: (1) civilian models and (2) racing boats.

THE CIVILIAN, OFF-THE-RACK GO-FASTS

Although there are a few small, elite companies that devote themselves almost exclusively to the manufacture of superfast boats, many of the stock high-performance vessels you see screaming by you on the water come from big companies with high-performance divisions.

True racing boats, like this racing catamaran, sacrifice comfort for eyeball-jiggling speed. Cats are particularly fast in flat water and are the most popular hull shape in professional racing today.

© Allan Weitz

Most of the boats from these divisions have hull shapes that, in a very general way, are probably not much different than what you'll find on runabouts. Go-fast hulls are usually modified-Vs, although deep-Vs, with their phenomenal ability to master heavy seas, are also popular.

Want to get a feel for what go-fasts are all about? Take a look at the steering console of a high-performance boat sometime. Notice the wheel. It's probably special. A symbol of sorts. A totem, leather bound, made in Italy. The kind of thing you see on an imported automobile. A very fast one.

At first blush, neophytes may suspect that the touted virtues of speed on the water is pure advertising hype. Do people really need Bertini steering wheels on boats? They will discover, however, should someone take them for a ride, that seventy miles (112 km) per hour in an open boat feels like about two hundred miles (320 km) per hour in a car. And yes, the leather on the wheel is a very good idea.

I've driven racing boats to speeds in excess of 115 miles (184 km) per hour (see chapter 8 for the details). It's amazing, at such speeds, how little one sees of the water and sky ahead. The view doesn't come at you in a linear, logical way, as it does in a car on land. Rather, it comes in flashes, like separate photographs bursting upon the mind's eye...blink, blink, blink.

Manufacturers lavish so much attention on the steering wheels of speedboats because they represent the mechanism of control. And that's the crux of speed: control. I once sat in a high-class eatery in Connecticut's Mystic Seaport with a man who literally invested millions of dollars buying, selling, and restoring Gold Cup racing boats. Having compared notes over a couple of excellent

The steering station of a modern high-performance sportboat certainly derives much from the automobile and airplane.

© Allan Weitz

hamburgers on the maximum speed we'd ever driven a boat, we began to talk about high speed, and how some people get addicted to it.

"I'll tell you what it is." He smiled at last, and stared off toward the front windows and the sunlight gleaming on the water beyond. He looked almost inspired. "It's being in control and almost out of control...all in the same split second. That's the attraction of speed."

By learning to use the wheel of a high-performance boat, as well as its throttles and shifts, you can place yourself at the exact same spot that Gold Cup goner was talking about. You can be on the edge of control, feeling the boat's trajectory change with only a slight, imperceptible movement of your wrist.

Very few people make their first boat a high-performance model. They prefer to develop their driving technique a bit. There is little room for error at high speeds.

Often advertised as a competition-type dashboard, the typical backdrop to the racing-type steering wheel on a high-performance boat is an array of gauges and indicators that let the driver know, at a glance, how his engines are faring, and whether his trim tabs and drives need adjusting. We'll get into all this terminology shortly in our discussion of racing boats.

Besides the dashboard, which is often vaguely reminiscent of that of a fighter plane, racing bolsters are also often found aboard many high-performance boats. If the boat is equipped with bolsters, the operator can drive the boat either standing up or sitting down, although the former is preferred because it gives the operator a better view.

The racing bolster is a type of very comfortable wraparound seat, with a bottom that folds down, either mechanically or electrically. Either way, by holding the body tight within its grasp, the bolster makes bearable the pounding, jolting, and vibrating sensations characteristic of most high-speed rides.

One final point. Accommodations on a high-performance boat, even a big, expensive one that costs more than a big, expensive trawler, are skimpy. You can figure this out by looking at the exterior of the boat. A high-performance boat is built like a needle. From the waterline up, the shape of the boat is as aerodynamic as that of an airplane. Below, the hull is as hydrodynamic as a dolphin.

Also, there is no superstructure, not even a windshield on many models. Instead of a flared bow, to keep spray from becoming a problem for the occupants, the hull at the bow is slab sided; as straight up and down as a tall apartment building. Some speedboats even have "reverse sheer" in their bows, meaning that, in profile, their noses are slightly aquiline. This shape makes them less likely to suffer from too much lift, which can cause the dreaded "blow-over" (meaning that the air rushing under the bow lifts it so far up that the boat actually does a somersault).

The aero- and hydrodynamism of the typical high-performance boat leaves little room for living space inside. Most have a V-berth forward, followed up by some type of seating arrangement amidships, with a small galley aft, and possibly an enclosed head. If a person is willing to sacrifice between $200,000

© Christopher Bain

There are all sorts of fast boats. While stern-drive configurations are probably the most popular, outboard power has its place in motorboating, too.

and $300,000 for a thirty-odd-footer (9 m) that'll do eighty miles (128 km) an hour, he will certainly have no qualms about sacrificing a little privacy.

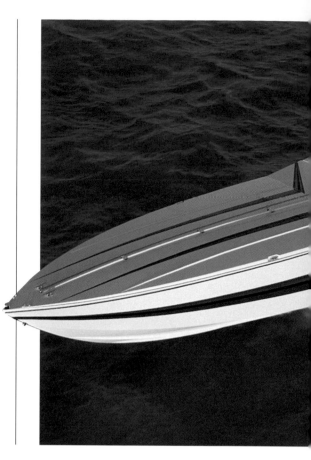

LEAN, MEAN, RACING MACHINES

There are two types of racing boats in use today: the deep-V and the racing catamaran. With some notable exceptions, the design and construction of most modern racing boats owe much, or even all, of their being to a crazy, ramshackle old street in North Miami, Florida, that became known during the 1970s and early 1980s as Thunderboat Row. Both types of racing boats are still built there, by several separate companies that were the brainchildren of the same man, Don Aronow.

Aronow dominated both the racing and manufacture of offshore speedboats for more than a decade, until his mysterious murder in 1987. He took the deep-V concept developed by C. Raymond Hunt in the early 1960s and honed it down to a fare-thee-well. By the time of his death, he'd probably developed and built more fast boats than any other human being on the planet.

In the beginning, Aronow built deep-Vs only. But later, in the 1970s and early 1980s, he began building racing catamarans for United States Customs for service in drug interdiction. We'll talk specifically about Aronow's famous cat-

amaran—Blue Thunder—in a moment; let's discuss the racing catamaran in general first.

To begin with, any catamaran consists of two bananalike hulls, connected by a transverse web at the top. The tunnel beneath the web between the hulls runs the length of the vessel. Why design a boat this way? First, the movement of air through the tunnel causes lift, reduces friction and water resistance, and increases speed. Second, a catamaran is normally wider than a monohull boat, so it's more stable, like a Polynesian dugout with an outrigger. Third, because of the bottom configuration, there is less draft, which means less drag. The result is a double-hulled screamer that, in fairly smooth sea conditions, has less wetted surface (hull area below the waterline), less drag, more lift and more speed than a deep-V, at least in theory. But in rough sea conditions, the deep-V's knifelike bottom gives it an advantage over a cat. Cats tend to pound in heavy seas and must be slowed down.

Aronow's Blue Thunder cat was a work of genius. Basically, it was a deep-V hull, split right down the middle and pulled apart a little bit. With a narrower tunnel, it was slower than other cats, but still quite stable and very maneuverable. The United States Customs service bought something like a dozen of them. Most are still in service. Drivers prefer them to the more traditional cat because, while they are comparatively slow, they handle rough water almost as well as deep-Vs.

RACING BOAT MOTORS

We can't finish our discussion of offshore racing boats without a word about engines. Actually, in gasoline-alley parlance, spoken in speed shops from Via Reggio to North Miami, the propulsion package of an offshore racer is called "the motors." Sport boats and civilian high-performance boats are ordinarily powered by pairs of stock engines from one of several manufacturers.

With offshore racing boats, it's a different story. Their engines are usually custom made, or at least customized to some degree. Many boats have three engines instead of two, although this approach may have some drawbacks. A third engine adds extra horsepower, but also adds weight, both of itself and in the extra fuel load it requires.

Brunswick Marine Power, which around the world is more familiarly known as Mercury Marine, supplies many of the high-performance engines to builders who use them "as is," or increase the horsepower by adding superchargers or turbochargers. The most outrageous engine setup I've ever seen was aboard a thirty-two-foot (8.2-m) Skater Cat called *Recovery*. She had a set of Lightning Performance engines, 848 horsepower apiece. Couple this kind of oomph with a light catamaran hull and you've got a boat that can do 130 miles (208 km) per hour almost effortlessly.

The deep-V raceboat (top), with its ability to slice through the waves, has the advantage in rough-water races. Racing hydroplanes (left) are often powered by custom engines.

FISHING BOATS, GREAT AND SMALL

Fishing for sailfish on big battlewagons in exotic locations is probably as exciting a sport as there is. It's also a little esoteric. You can have just as much fun with smaller boats. One of the most revered names in big-game sportfishing, John Rybovich, says he often prefers to fish in small boats, with fairly primitive tackle, because the connection between himself and his catch seems more elemental. These are the words of a builder of some of the most spectacular sportfishing boats ever to grace the Gulf Stream.

Most marinas today contain many more small fishing boats than large ones. Small fishing boats are usually either of two types: center consoles or cuddies. The center-console sportfishing vessel is basically an open boat, with a cockpit that runs unobstructed from bow to stern. In the middle of this cockpit is a fiberglass module with a steering and control station and usually two adjustable seats or a leaning post. Hull shapes vary. Although they're not built expressly for speed, some center-console sportfishing boats are very fast. Take it from a guy who ran aground in one, in Sarasota Bay, Florida, one evening, at roughly (and I do mean roughly) sixty miles (96 km) per hour.

The other type of small fishing boat, the cuddy-cabin model, is a little more versatile, in that it can be cruised. The control station is located on the bulkhead that separates the cockpit aft from the little cabin forward, which usually contains a V-berth and perhaps a portable toilet, or head.

Small fishing boats, or comparatively small ones (opposite), have most of the fish-fighting gear that the battlewagons do, such as fancy rod stowage (left).

© Allan Weitz

Both kinds of fishing boats are often loaded with special equipment, and quite a few of them, at least the ones that are built to travel offshore, are powered with two engines, for safety's sake.

You can spend literally thousands of dollars adding fishing-related equipment to a twenty-six-foot (7.8-m) boat. In addition to the rod racks under the gunwales, livewells, and fishboxes, which are standard features, you can buy brackets of rod holders called "rocket launchers," T-tops for shade, fighting chairs and posts, and electronic gadgets ad infinitum.

If trawlers get first place in the competition for my fickle heart, large sportfishing boats place a close second. And by big, I mean anything from thirty-footers (9 m) to the giants, with seventy feet (21 m) or more of waterline length. The reason I'm fond of these boats is that although they are certainly built for recreation, they are also built to do a job. This keeps them honest and functional.

You can see the honesty and function in the shape. A big sportfishing boat is all clean efficiency and simplicity, like a shark. The bows are high, with lots of flare and flam to beat spray back into the ocean. The cockpit is low to facilitate working a marlin, a sail, or a giant tuna in close to the transom, or maybe even bringing the fish into the cockpit for the kill, although that sort of thing has become rather passé. Fortunately, most sportfishermen today release their catches.

Unlike center consoles or cuddies, big sportfishing boats are built to take the worst conditions Mother Nature can dish out. Most are good sea boats, and they have to be. Pursuit of the quarry may require anything from trips to the famous "canyons" a hundred or more miles (160 or more km) off the New Jersey coast to voyages around the world. After all, marlin cannot be fished from armchairs. They live in such places as the Gulf Stream, the coasts of South America, Central America, Africa, and Australia.

The svelte look of a battlewagon's exterior often belies an interior that, in terms of creature comfort, will rival a penthouse suite at the Ritz Carlton. The owners of big sportfishing boats, or at least some of them, are most definitely a breed apart.

At the Bahia Mar in Fort Lauderdale, where the Dusenbergs outnumber the Mercedes in the parking lot, I stepped aboard a multimillion-dollar vessel a couple of years ago with the intention of interviewing its owner on the subject of some marine-related matter. After removing my shoes so as not to dirty the teak covering boards on the cockpit coamings, I hopped into a coliseumlike cockpit and headed for a door of carved teak that led into the interior.

Once inside, I discovered the owner, a Houston businessman, in the salon, wearing a bathing suit, a diamond-studded Rolex, and a pair of Wayfarers. He was smoking a cigarette, sitting on a settee upholstered with alligator hide, and talking animatedly on a cellular phone.

"Lookee here," he drawled, like a typical character in a Louis L'Amour novel. "You tell him if I like it, maybe I'll just swing a couple million bucks' wortha business his way."

Sportfishermen come in all shapes and sizes, from trendy, comfort-conscious Palm Beachers (opposite) to hard-core, center-console anglers (above).

BORN TO CRUISE

I suppose the first man that set forth upon the water had that look in his eye. The kind of look you might imagine would have been in the eyes of the great explorers. Almost everyone, especially today, feels the need occasionally to be removed from the stress of life. To get away. Have an adventure. One of the best ways, maybe even one of the few remaining ways, is to take a motorboat cruise.

Your cruise may last a weekend or a week, or even two weeks. Regardless of the duration, your cruise is bound to share similarities with all other cruises, past and present. For starters, you will get to know the people aboard your boat a lot better. This can be good or bad, depending on how much you want to better acquaint yourself with your crew in the first place. And cruising is a wonderful family pastime, but be careful about who else you invite along.

Approaching a place from the water is a much different experience than approaching it from land. Why? It just is. I'd venture to say that if you were able to visit your own hometown by cruising motorboat, you'd find out all sorts of things about the place you never knew before. In fact, you discover many new things while cruising—about yourself, and the people and the world around you.

There's one more benefit of motorboat cruising: peace of mind. The long, lazy days in the sun, meals at goofy waterside eateries and occasional posh restaurants, stops on deserted coves and beaches, the mist on the water in the morning, all these things have a cumulative effect. You'll forget about your worries and one hundred million obligations at home, and you'll shake loose the tyranny of the television, the radio, the newspapers and magazines.

Cruisers, more than any other type of boat, vary in size. Motoryachts, for example, can be almost as big as ships. They make their elegant passages with the assistance of hired crews and captains. They may contain accommodations for a dozen guests and enough extra room for huge parties.

The majority of cruising boats are about forty feet (12 m) long. Generally, they are not built to cross oceans. Their designers had vacationing and voyaging more in mind. A good cruising boat always has plenty of well-distributed stowage areas. Without them, the interior will always look like a bombed-out haberdashery, with clothing and small items of gear strewn about haphazardly.

I spent a couple of weeks, some years ago, cruising down the Saint Lawrence River with my two children on an "aft cabin" motorboat that had plenty of stowage room. There was a place for everything and everything was in its place.

Besides stowage, the boat had plenty of privacy for everybody aboard, whether we were under way, at anchor, or at the dock. There was a stateroom forward, with a V-shaped berth, another stateroom aft, with its own head. A large salon, which was raised to accommodate the twin engines beneath it, was in the middle. The galley, with its full-size refrigerator, two-burner cooking surface, and deep stainless-steel sink was adequate for our cooking needs, and the berths were comfortable. The trip went smoothly because the boat had been designed smoothly.

Some boats are born to cruise. Others have cruising as well as fishing potential.

I ALWAYS WANTED A DARN TRAWLER

I remember a similar trip that did not go as well. The boat was poorly designed. There was little stowage for clothing or stores, and less privacy. Nobody had time enough to have a good time. We were all having to constantly go through piles of paraphernalia in order to sort our T-shirts from the breakfast food.

If you can't afford a forty-foot (12-m) cruiser, don't despair. Hard-core cruising enthusiasts are not so much limited by the size of the boat, or its cost, as by the size of their imaginations. You don't need a forty-footer (12 m) to have a good time. When I was younger, I took a very enjoyable cruise of a couple of weeks in a nineteen-foot (5.7-m) shallow draft, flat-bottomed fiberglass boat. Amenities consisted of a couple of sleeping bags, a small tent, and a Styrofoam cooler. We docked in a different port every night. Although that cruise was confined to a short segment of Lake Ontario, it was every bit as exciting, exotic, and relaxing as any cruise I've taken since. To the skeptic who suggests that the pleasures of the trip were in part due to my youth, I have just one thing to say: I am right now planning a longer but similar trip, in a similar vessel.

The shapes of cruising boats vary as much as the size. You probably cannot conceive of a reasonable cruising boat that has not already been built, but you probably can conceive of some unreasonable ones that already have. Smaller boats, or sport cruisers, usually have planing hulls. Larger boats have displacement or semidisplacement hulls. A catalog from almost any major boat builder will typically contain a dozen cruising boats alone, from twenty-six (7.8 m) to sixty (18 m) feet in length.

Cruising is a varied pastime. For megayachters and big-boat enthusiasts, sometimes the best way to get ashore is in a rigid-bottom inflatable (below). Buy an old family cruiser (opposite) and go ashore in a plywood dinghy; it's just as much fun.

Like almost any other human endeavor, motorboating has its wacky side, an aspect that mosies along to the beat of a different drummer. There are all kinds of "different" conveyances out there today that may be loosely construed as motorboats. At the present time, for a very healthy sum, you can purchase your own personal submarine. Its electric motor runs on rechargeable batteries. It's small. One-man and two-man versions are available.

I ALWAYS WANTED A DARN TRAWLER

Here are some other ways to cruise: the wet and wild Personal Water Vehicle (top), and the easy-living, coastal-cruising houseboat (bottom).

You can also buy your own hovercraft. Hovercraft ride over the waves, swamps, and even sandy beaches (for a short distance at least) on a cushion of air created by fans. Propulsion is provided by air or water propellers. Calm weather is required and, in many cases, so are ear protectors. Given the engine noise some models make, personal hovercraft should travel at close to the speed of light. They don't, however.

Another invention gaining in popularity is the personal water vehicle, or PWV. Shaped something like a snowmobile and about the same size, it relies on engine-powered water-jet propulsion, since spinning propellers could prove dangerous to a driver. Personal water vehicles are sometimes carried as adjuncts to larger vessels. Water toys, if you will. Single-operator versions are the most common.

Let's wind up this chapter with mention of two boat types that are "different" but eminently practical. Because of its boxlike shape, the houseboat offers more living room per foot of waterline length than just about any other type. Houseboats are not built for oceans, but for living aboard and cruising inland waterways and coasts. They represent a lot of boat for the money.

Small fiberglass tugboats are fairly popular on Long Island Sound and in the Great Northwest. Some people like the way they look. They don't care that the little vessels resemble real tugboats, which, because of their high super-structures and round bottoms, have a tendency to roll wickedly. You can buy miniature tugs in various sizes. Because they are roomy, picturesque, and quite seaworthy, they are cruised extensively. Some folks live aboard, too.

Another cruising option — tour the country in a nifty little cruising tug, made of fiberglass instead of steel. With a diesel engine, you can expect superb fuel efficiency.

CHAPTER THREE

MODERN MARINE PROPULSION SYSTEMS

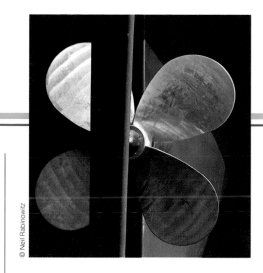

© Neil Rabinowitz

One afternoon, about one hundred miles (160 km) offshore, a small runabout with a single engine pulled up alongside the tug/supply vessel I was working on at the time. We were hanging off a mooring buoy, hard by an oil rig, waiting to offload a few hundred tons (270 t) of drill pipe. The appearance of this runabout, bobbing along the starboard side of a two-hundred-foot (60-m) supply boat, was a little mind-boggling. A hundred miles (160 km) offshore is a long way for a runabout to travel. Too far, I'd say, even on one of those summer days when the Gulf of Mexico is slick calm.

"You guys got any gas?" yelled the skipper of the runabout, revealing in a few words that his general knowledge of boats and seafaring was scant and that he and his crew had no business being where they presently were.

"No, we burn diesel fuel," I explained. "The nearest gas is the Chevron station in Cameron, Louisiana."

WHAT'LL IT BE, GAS OR DIESEL?

There's little point in recounting the rest of the tale. I only bring it up to make a point: The majority of modern marine engines run on either of two types of fuel, gasoline or diesel. No matter how desperate you are, the two don't mix. And they can't be interchanged, at least in most engines.

Another rule of thumb to remember, should you stray off course and get low on fuel due to the proximity of a pocketknife to your magnetic compass, is that basically, big boats burn diesel, small boats burn gas, and middle-sized boats may burn either.

It's true that diesel fuel is safer than gas. If it weren't, all the crazy old engineers I've known who thought nothing of lighting up a cigarette or cigar while pumping diesel fuel would have blown themselves up, with an oily rag in their back pockets and quizzical looks on their faces.

© courtesy OMC

Generally speaking, most modern outboards have gasoline engines. Diesel outboards are fairly scarce.

Certainly, I'm not recommending that anyone be so utterly unconcerned about their own safety and the safety of others as to smoke, create sparks, or do anything else of an inflammatory nature in the presence of diesel fumes. It's just that under ordinary circumstances, diesel is not explosive, which is definitely one of its advantages as a motorboating fuel.

Diesels have other advantages, too. Per given horsepower rating, a diesel is a tougher, heavier-built engine than a gasoline engine, although traditionally diesels turn slower, develop less speed, and have less acceleration. A diesel has to be tougher. The explosions that operate its pistons are brought about by compression, not spark plugs. The engine must be able to withstand the pressure of this compression.

Weight differences between diesel and gas engines used to be quite dramatic. Gas had the advantage. Today, the differential is narrowing. I know of at least two high-performance or speedboat builders who have seen fit to install diesels. The weight-to-horsepower ratios were that good. One of the builders, a Japanese gentleman, installs diesels exclusively, and some of his boats are capable of speeds in excess of 100 miles (160 km) per hour.

Most marine engines, whether gas or diesel, are landlubbers in disguise. A company, such as Brunswick Marine Power (MerCruiser) or OMC (Outboard Motor Corporation), buys basic engine components from General Motors or Ford, then creates a version that will withstand the marine environment. Where most marinized gasoline engines originate with automobile manufacturers, however, diesels usually come from builders of trucks, heavy equipment, even locomotives.

Industrial and commercial interests choose the diesel engine for their vessels for its strength and endurance. To develop a given amount of horsepower, a diesel operates at a much lower rpm (revolutions per minute) than a gasoline engine. Less rpm means less wear and tear. With proper maintenance and care, a diesel will last longer than a gas engine and probably require less service. Even if it's treated badly, a diesel may still live a much longer life, and a much more resolute life, than a gasoline engine.

Once a chief engineer and I were standing in a large and complex engine room, between a pair of twenty-cylinder Electro-Motive-Diesels (EMDs)—the same sort of diesels used to power locomotives—marveling at how one of them had run for several hours without benefit of water pumps, which supply a necessary cooling effect. True, the damage to the engine had been cat-astrophic, but it had not been terminal. The chief, who could afford to wax philosophical, since the accident was the fault of another chief engineer who had just recently been relieved of his duties, said: "It's amazing, ain't it? This big, dumb ol' engine. Long as she's got air, she'll live. Starve her for water. Even starve her for oil. She just won't give up. Wish my wives was like that."

Despite the advantages of the diesel, gasoline engines dominate the marine marketplace today. Gasoline engines for boats dominate in countries where gas engines dominate the automotive field. One of the best reasons to own a boat with gasoline engines in America or Great Britain is their popularity. Their sheer numbers make them cheap.

MODERN MARINE PROPULSION SYSTEMS

Gasoline is explosive— much more so than diesel fuel. In many cases, diesel fuel will not even burn when subjected to the direct contact of a burning match. Gasoline, and more particularly its fumes, will of course react much differently.

There are some other reasons to have a boat with a gasoline engine. Basically, it's usually much easier to get parts, and to have service done and repairs effected. The only exception is the modern, gasoline-powered outboard. Because modular electronic components are used in many of these models, repairs tend to be expensive. Often, the failure of a small part dictates the replacement of an entire module. In addition, it's not unusual to discover that your local mechanic doesn't have the particular module he needs in stock. Then, of course, you both have to wait for the manufacturer to ship the module.

As mentioned earlier, gasoline engines are less expensive than diesels, partly because there are so many of them on the market, partly because they're not as heavily built, inside or out.

Gasoline engines in motorboats are quite safe, as long as the operator follows certain rules:

1) Before fueling, shut down engines and the electrical system (including motors, fans, and anything else that might cause a spark) and make sure galley fires are out. Don't smoke. Have a fire extinguisher close at hand.

2) While fueling, so there's no chance of sparks, make sure the nozzle stays in constant contact with the fill opening of your boat. Don't overfill your tanks. Allow for expansion of the fuel with temperature changes. Allowing fuel to flow from tank vents is in poor environmental taste and, on top of that, it's very dangerous.

3) After fueling, sniff the bilge. Ventilate your boat for three or four minutes, and open all ports and hatches. Don't rely on fume detectors or any other means of determining whether there are gasoline fumes in the bottom of the boat. The bottom line: Start your engines only when your nose tells you it's safe to do so.

It used to be that gasoline was more expensive than diesel fuel. This is much less so today, when in most places the difference in price is a matter of cents. But bear in mind that a gasoline engine is generally less fuel efficient than a diesel engine, so it really costs quite a bit more to feed. Although you'll have a hard time buying it from tugboats on the high seas, gasoline is available at most conventional fuel docks. In some instances, diesel is not.

So which is better? Gas or diesel? To begin with, some boats are too small or inexpensive to warrant diesels. Nobody in their right mind is going to install a set of high-priced Caterpillar or Detroit Diesels in a low-priced puddle jumper. Sure, diesels are installed in some runabouts, but these boats are generally of the very special—translate, expensive—variety and often do duty as tenders to diesel-powered megayachts.

By the same token, gasoline engines are seldom, if ever, found in megayachts. The cost of such vessels and the ranges they typically cruise at call for the employment of the most dependable, long-term, and fuel-efficient approach to propulsion possible.

So, at least with runabouts and megayachts, size basically dictates the type of fuel; this leaves large numbers of vessels that can take either type. Safety may play some part in an owner's decision to install gas- or diesel-powered engines in his medium-sized cruiser, but the biggest concern is usually cost. Is the higher initial cost of the diesel warranted, based on the projected savings in maintenance and fuel consumption, as well as the probable higher resale value? The answer basically depends on how long the motorboatman intends to keep his boat, and how steadily he hopes to use it. Generally, a three-weekend-a-year motorboatman will likely choose gas. The person who's out on the water every chance he gets will choose diesel.

DIFFERENT STROKES FOR DIFFERENT BOATS: INBOARDS AND OUTBOARDS

Gas or diesel, there are several types of modern marine engine installations. The most tried and true propulsion system is the inboard. The term means that the entire power package (engine, reduction gear, clutches, etc.) is inside the vessel. Outside are the shafts, propellers, and rudders. Ships have inboard-type propulsion systems.

THE INBOARD: THE OLD STANDBY

The inboard used to be the most conventional sort of configuration in marine power trains, even in smaller boats. This isn't true anymore. (I've tested and written about an awful lot of small to medium-sized motorboats. Only the very largest of them have been inboards.)

Because most commercial and large recreational vessels are inboards, it seems reasonable to assume that, while the setup may not have a lot of sparkle, it's still practical, cost effective, and durable for big-boat applications. Inboards also make excellent fishing boats as the running gear (propellers, rudders, etc.) is under the boat, where it can't interfere with fishing lines or hauling a big fish over the transom.

A naval architect may opt for an inboard power package for design reasons, particularly if that package contains what is known as the V-drive. Although it's somewhat complicated to explain, the V-drive is really a fairly simple device, a common adjunct to many inboard engine installations. Basically, a V-drive unit is a space saver. To incorporate one into a drive train, the engine is turned around, so the front is facing aft in the machinery spaces. The drive shaft, which would normally lead aft, leads forward instead, to the V-drive unit. Another longer shaft leading aft from the V-drive unit passes under the engine and exits the hull in the conventional manner. In profile, the configurations of the two shafts and the V-Drive form a V-shaped drive train. Hence the name.

Because they make it possible to locate an inboard engine further aft and lower in the hull, V-drives are often used in medium-sized cruisers to free up otherwise unusable interior space to create more room for accommodations. About the only drawback is the power loss in the drive itself, which is caused by friction.

Barring some smaller, high-performance ski boats, which seek to improve weight distribution and increase pulling performance with inboard automobile engines, and a few high-toned gentleman's runabouts as well, most inboard boats these days are at least thirty feet (9 m) long. Over forty feet (12 m), almost all conventionally driven boats are inboard powered.

There are a couple of reasons why this is so. First of all, the inboard configuration is strong enough to handle big engines, those that are larger than the engines you normally find in smaller boats. And secondly, it's primarily in bigger boats that the advantages of the inboard configuration—

courtesy U.S. Marine

Regardless of engine configuration, most boats can serve a number of purposes. The little runabout shown above is both a sleep-aboard minicruiser and a surprisingly powerful skiboat.

such as conventionality and compatibility with big horsepower—outweigh the disadvantages.

Here's a quick example to illustrate this point. Except for changing propellers, an inboard drive train cannot be easily adjusted or modified, either under way or at the dock. This is a comparative disadvantage since, in some of the power packages we'll talk about later, the angle at which the propeller confronts the water can be easily changed, thus effecting a change in the attitude of the boat even while it's running. Often, if you can readily change a boat's running attitude, you can make it plane faster and run more efficiently. This is just about always true, at least when you're talking about small boats.

An older type of power configuration, the inboard system was found on the "gentleman's runabouts" (below) that were popular during the earlier half of this century.

MODERN MARINE PROPULSION SYSTEMS

Before moving on to a discussion of the modern outboard, let's take a look at what may be a myth: Two engines are better than one. There's no particular reason to examine this theorem in light of inboard power configurations. It could be scrutinized just as easily elsewhere, since it's been applied to just about every type of engine. But old and moldy beliefs often address fundamental concerns that should be dealt with early on, so here goes.

First, is the two-engine installation really safer than the single? It's often argued that offshore anglers and other far rangers should have two engines, an extra in case one quits. Does the argument hold water?

A friend of mine, a fellow boating writer and ex-U.S. Coast Guard captain, has been messing about in boats for fifty years. He thinks the theory that two engines are safer than one is "a bunch of baloney." He even goes so far as to suggest that the single engine may actually be safer. Why? His reasoning sounds a little extreme at first. But once you hear him out, you feel the ring of truth, probably because his ideas are based on the close observation of humanity, both at sea and ashore.

My friend's thinking, to which I heartily subscribe, goes something like this. Because our society is so busy and preoccupied with all sorts of things, from cholesterol counts to cable TV, we have only a certain amount of time to devote to boating. It is sad but true.

Also, we have an even smaller amount of time to devote to engine maintenance, and that amount will remain pretty much constant, whether we choose a single engine or decide to buy a boat with twins.

Even the modern boatman who promises to double the amount of time he spends keeping everything shipshape down in the greasy old engine room, upon exchanging a well-maintained single for a twin, is setting himself up for trouble. His extra-boating affairs continue apace and, despite the best intentions, the modern motorboatman's twin-engine maintenance schedule goes to hell in a mop bucket. There's barely enough time to keep one engine watered and fed. Two's too much. The moral of the tale? One properly cared-for engine is much more reliable than two.

There's another point in favor of single-engine installations. We've already dealt with the handling problems associated with single-engine inboards, particularly when operating astern, in chapter 2. Such problems are not usually encountered in other types of "transom-powered" installations, like outboards and stern drives. Since these types can be more or less aimed in the direction the driver wants to go, astern or otherwise, a single transom-powered engine is just about as easy to back up as a twin although, certainly, a set of counter-rotating twins obviates the need to compensate for torque bias.

One last point. Many inboard boats have hulls with shallow, thick fins running along the centerlines. This fin is called a skeg or sometimes a keel. Often, at least in single-engine inboards, the propeller is positioned at the rear of the skeg or thereabouts and is protected by it in the event of a grounding. Propellers on twin-engine inboards are found on either side of the skeg and are protected by it to a much lesser extent, if they are protected at all.

Are two engines really better than one? For most owners of large sport cruisers, the question is a moot one. Manufacturers usually install twin engines in such boats anyway, to improve speed and handling.

© Allar Weitz

THE OUTBOARD...LIGHTWEIGHT CHAMPION OF THE WORLD

The light bulb went on over Ole Evinrude's head one hot, muggy afternoon around 1903 as he dripped sweat and bravely plied a set of oars in his rowboat on Okauchee Lake in the Midwest. His idea was not entirely new. The Germans had already built an outboard motor; a ponderous thing, heavy and impractical. Another firm had tried, too, but failed just as miserably.

Word of such oddball inventions scarcely penetrated the backwoods of Dane County, Wisconsin, where Evinrude grew up, at least not during the very early twentieth century. It's not likely that Ole's invention was much inspired by the work of other earlier mechanical engineers, either.

But there was a girl, Bess Cary, and she wanted some ice cream. That's how passionate but shy Ole got to thinking about outboards.

Ole announced that he would fetch the ice cream at a store across Okauchee in his rowboat. That meant two miles (3.2 km) over and two miles back.

For outboard boats, a good solution to the single versus twin-engine controversy is the use of a big outboard for long runs and a smaller "kicker" that can be used for trolling and in emergencies.

Rowing back across the lake against the wind, Ole was forced to witness the melting of the ice cream. He watched the lovely and mountainous vanilla crags soften, begin to sink into an encircling pool, and finally liquefy.

This, Ole told himself, would not happen again. He would build a gasoline motor, toggle it up somehow to a propeller, and attach the whole apparatus to the back of a boat.

Bess ate the melted ice cream anyway. Ole asked her to marry him, and she said yes. Time passed.

In April of 1909, Ole and his brother-in-law, Russ Cary, carried an extraordinary contraption through the streets of Madison, Wisconsin, to the shores of the Kinnickinnic River. They rented an old tub for fifty cents, affixed the first Evinrude to ever grace a transom, and cranked her up.

A bunch of deckhands on some nearby Great Lakes coal carriers waved and yelled as the tub chugged bravely across the greasy Kinnickinnic. The contraption worked. And so the outboard motor was born.

My first outboard was a one-and-a-half-horsepower Sea King handed down to me by my grandfather. It had been handed down to him by Montgomery Ward, in exchange for less money than what a tuna-fish sandwich costs in a Manhattan delicatessen today.

The Sea King was perfect for Gramps because it was lightweight. Since he kept his boat a fair distance from the house, chained to a willow tree that grew down along the Oswegatchie River, and since the Sea King was stored in the cellar, at the bottom of a long set of steps, along with some old cans of oil and gas (which had to be mixed in exact alchemical proportions), any motorized fishing trip Gramps took called for considerable toting.

Another advantage of the Sea King, besides being lightweight, was its compactness. Gramps didn't have a lot of room, either on his transom or down in his cellar, which was crowded with fishing and hunting paraphernalia, tools, buckets of bolts, nuts, screws and nails, a wood furnace, firewood, a cistern for water, and hundreds of mason jars full of pickles, berries, and vegetables from his garden. In fact, these two attributes—light weight and comparatively small size—are the biggest reasons for the modern outboard's popularity.

In Gramp's day, the outboard was about as reliable as a granny knot. Oil and gas had to be mixed by hand, and if the proportions were off just a tad, either of two unhappy scenarios would ensue. Too much oil meant excess smoke, and once the plugs had been thoroughly fouled, the motor coughed, choked, and died. Too little oil caused a condition analagous to what happens when some hapless motorist tries driving his or her car without the proper amount of oil in the crankcase. The outboard would spring to life when cranked, thriving on the properly mixed liquid remaining in the carburetor. Then, starving for oil, it would begin to overheat. Eventually, it might even seize.

Except for a boy and his dog, there's nothing quite so inseparable as a boy and his Sea King.

The process of starting an old-fashioned outboard was often difficult and physically demanding. It involved either a spring-loaded starter cord on the pricey models or a simple rope, with a wooden handle at one end and a knot at the other, with which the motorboatman spun the flywheel on top of the power head. (One of the real drawbacks of being a passenger in an old-fashioned outboard-powered skiff was having to duck the knotted end of the cord when it went flying through the air after each attempted start.)

Most outboards these days start electrically, with the flick of a switch. They are very reliable and can be purchased in V-4, V-6, and V-8 configurations worldwide. Some models even deliver preprogrammed, spoken messages to tell you if an oil line is clogged or your safety lanyard—a cord the driver can attach to himself that will stop the engine if he is accidentally thrown from the boat—is disconnected.

Some outboards will automatically reduce their own engine rpm if the flow of cooling water is interrupted for any reason. They are electronically fuel-injected, loop-charged, computer-controlled, exhaust-tuned miracles of modern science.

Outboards have other advantages. Their propeller angle can be adjusted, so the propellers confront the water head on no matter what the running attitude of the boat. In larger models, this angle can be changed under way, by simply pushing the "trim" switch contained in the throttle/shift control handle or mounted on the dashboard. The motor is adjusted via hydraulic rams actuated by a tiny electric motor. On some smaller engines, the adjustment must still be made by hand, after the boat has been stopped. The power head is simply tilted up with one hand, and a minor adjustment made to the transom bracket with the other.

The fact that an outboard is normally mounted outside the boat is another major advantage. With the motor outside, there's much more room inside the boat for tackle boxes, stowage compartments, seating, rod holders, and passengers.

The drawback here is quite obvious: you've got a big lump of metal, or two big lumps of metal (if you're a twin-engine motorboatman), hanging off the transom, getting in the way. Some people distance themselves from their motors a bit by hanging them on brackets that are attached to the transom but extend well abaft it. This makes the propellers more efficient by putting them in less turbulent water at speed, but it doesn't resolve the problem. Outboards can be a distinct handicap, especially for anglers in areas where downriggers are traditionally mounted at the stern. One other thing. It's easy to tangle a fishing line up in an outboard and lose a fish nobody'll ever believe you had hooked. I speak from experience.

You want to buy an outboard? Although three-hundred-horsepower models are not uncommon, the majority of outboards for sale today are in the neighborhood of ten horsepower. The typical inboard, as well as the typical stern drive, is a four-cycle engine, just like the engines in most cars. Outboards, on the other hand, are two-cycle engines, which means that they are a little more troublesome.

Depending upon its size, the modern outboard motor can be rated for as much as three hundred or as little as one and a half horsepower. Most outboards are two-stroke engines, but cleaner-burning, four-stroke models have recently become available.

Just like Gramps's old Sea King, smaller modern outboards consume gasoline only if it's been precisely laced with oil. With some of the smaller motors, you still have to do this by hand, outside the engine. Frankly, this can be a pain in the neck.

But with big engines, life is simpler. The need to mix oil into the gas has all but been eliminated by building an oil reservoir into the boat itself. The operator simply fills the reservoir, which is fed into the engine, where it is mixed with the fuel, automatically and precisely.

Many manufacturers today offer boats that can be purchased either with outboards or some other configuration, usually stern drives. If you're faced with the choice, your decision is going to basically depend upon the way you use your boat. Compare two boats, the same model, one with a stern-drive power package and the other with an outboard of equal horsepower. You're going to find that the retail price is about the same.

There are ways to make an outboard-powered boat look like it isn't an outboard. The advantage to the setup shown here is that the engine can be removed, even swapped for another, and the procedure is much easier to do than with other drive systems.

Generally speaking, outboards are faster, more powerful, and accelerate better than just about anything else, pound for pound. They are also much more reliable than they used to be.

But a modern outboard can be tougher to repair and maintain than a stern drive, given the computerized parts that may make up an outboard. If you understand automobile engines, simple ones like those your grandfather used to own, you're probably going to have a pretty good understanding of your inboard or your stern drive. There's no such guarantee with an outboard. It may be wholly as complicated and mysterious as the computerized power plant under the hood of the typical imported Japanese car.

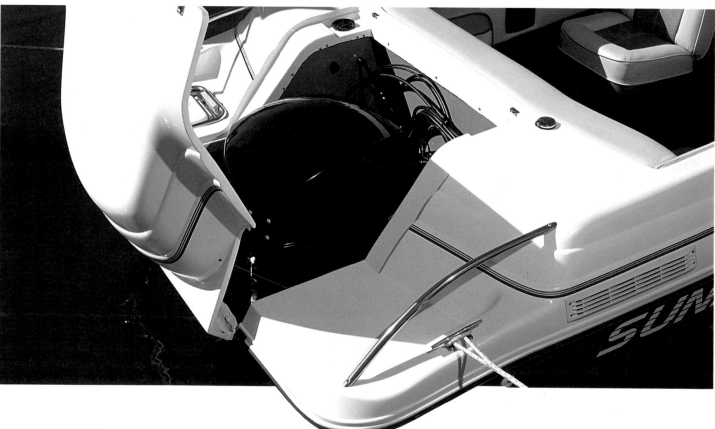

THE FAB CREATION OF MR. WYNN: THE INBOARD/ OUTBOARD ENGINE

Like any other stroke of genius, Jim Wynn's was a simple idea: Combine the advantages of the inboard power plant (low fuel consumption, four-cycle operation, protection from the elements, security from theft, long service, and high resale value) with the advantages of the outboard (integral propeller and shaft, propeller thrust parallel with boat's running attitude, easy repair of any underwater damage, extra living space because of a transom-mounted engine, low power loss in the transmission, and simple installation).

Prior to the 1950s, attempts to create a so-called inboard/outboard (I/O) had been unsuccessful. To some extent, this was due to technical difficulties in design and fabrication. To a larger extent, it was due to the fact that the I/O was looked upon as a gadget, installed at high prices in high-priced boats by nerdy inventor types. In a way, the ascendance of fiberglass at the close of the decade changed all this. People began building and buying more recreational boats than ever. The time was ripe for new developments.

Jim Wynn, a young mechanical engineer from Florida, is popularly credited with the invention of the stern drive in 1958, although Charlie Strang, a fellow Mercury Marine coworker, seems to be the true inventor. Having resigned as chief test engineer for Mercury a year earlier, Wynn had been working since then on an I/O project in his mother's garage. He was trying to connect a Volvo Penta inboard to a lower unit from a Mercury outboard.

Wynn was eventually successful, and a new stern-drive engine, the Volvo Penta Aquamatic, appeared at the New York Boat Show in 1959. Advertisements at the time promised the Aquamatic would match outboard speed at one-third the cost. The ads also pledged that motorboatmen would no longer have to mix oil, that the Aquamatic was quieter and safer than an outboard, and that it offered tilt protection under way and tilt convenience for beaching or trailering, just like an outboard. The I/O, or stern drive, was on its way to becoming a major force in motorboating. Today the stern drive can be found on runabouts, medium-sized cruisers, race boats, and sportfishing boats, either in single- or twin-engine installations around the world.

Like outboards, stern drives have advantages exclusive to themselves. One of the most important is the uniformity of construction that becomes possible when I/Os are part of the finished product. Other power configurations, particularly inboards, require a custom approach to installation.

Installing a self-contained I/O, however, is much easier than installing the rudders, shafts, stuffing boxes, and cutlass bearings that are part of an inboard arrangement. The assembly-line approach possible with I/Os saves money and time.

Where either type of installation is possible, I prefer the stern drive to the modern outboard. Perhaps this is because I grew up during an age of small and often unreliable outboards. I still distrust them. More likely it's because a stern drive, since it's basically a simple automobile engine, seems more familiar to

The Volvo Penta Aquamatic, which had its debut at the New York Boat Show in 1959, was the first workable stern drive to appear on the market.

Courtesy Volvo/Penta

me. Because it's located inside the boat, it's easier to work on and service, much easier than an outboard, which hangs off the transom.

I'm not alone in this. Some time ago, a friend of mine was planning a boating vacation on the western end of Lake Erie, among the islands of the little archipelago there. In the last few years, cleanup efforts on Lake Erie have made this area increasingly attractive to motorboatmen and anglers. The vessel that would carry my friend and his wife through some sun-and-fun-filled days was a sound one, a twenty-six-foot (7.8-m) fishing boat with a small but ample cuddy cabin. The boat was powered by a pair of brand-new, loop-charged, computerized, two-hundred-horsepower outboards with engine cowls that looked like modern art.

On departure morning, my friend and his wife loaded the boat, a considerable task. Then, with a grin of anticipation, my friend turned the ignition keys. Nothing. Neither outboard would crank. Because of the complexity of these machines, the unhappy couple had nary a clue as to what might be the problem and, instead of vacationing for seven days on the boat, spent the week waiting for a specialist to obtain and install a new computer chip.

Had the boat been stern-drive powered, there's a good chance my friend might have been able to fix it. Or maybe his wife could have. She knows a bit about automobile engines herself.

The last thing I'm going to say in praise of stern drives is that they're adaptable. A few manufacturers are offering standard stern-drive lower units outside the transom, with diesel engines inside the boat. Of course, purchase prices for these offbeat stern drives are high. But once installed, they'll offer owners all the long-term advantages associated with diesels.

UNCONVENTIONAL PROPULSION

In chapter 1, we looked at the evolution of the motorboat, as well as a number of fairly arcane methods of propulsion. The motorboatman's penchant for the arcane has apparently diminished over the years. There simply aren't that many bizarre propulsion systems kicking around anymore. Here are the only titillating types I can think of.

The first is the Arneson drive. In order to understand it, you have to understand surface-piercing propellers or propeller drives that are only partially submerged when running. Surface-piercing propellers date back to the early part of the twentieth century, when experimenters were just beginning to get some real, practical propulsion out of screw propellers in general. Until then, there had been little success. But, as I mentioned in chapter 1, the development of the internal-combustion engine in the early 1900s made it possible to turn propellers at much higher speeds than ever before. To apply the modifier *high-speed* to these early wheels would be to give antiquity a little more than its due. But let's do it anyway, for old time's sake.

From playing around with high-speed propellers, experimenters discovered several things. Much of the energy imparted to the propeller by the engine shaft is dissipated into the water, totally lost, in the form of friction. Friction is created between the water and the shaft itself, between the water and the strut, the device that supports the business end of the shaft, and between the water and the hub of the propeller.

They also learned that a propeller imparts most of its thrust to the water during less than half its full rotation. What I mean is this: Imagine one entire rotation of the propeller as the face of a clock. The lion's share of the propeller's

The wave of the future? Besides the unique drive systems mentioned here, the twenty-first century promises inboards, outboards, and stern drives that are cleaner and more fuel efficient than anything on the market today.

thrust is generated between the hours of two and five. Exactly why this is true is very complicated. If you've got a burning desire to know, you can read a detailed explanation of it in Robert Taggart's *Marine Propulsion—Principles and Evolution*.

So the idea that propeller efficiency could be improved by keeping a portion of the propeller out of the water was certainly not new. But it was unusable until 1980, when Howard Arneson developed a unit that didn't fall apart after a few minutes of operation. Heretofore, surface-piercing units, with shafts that exited straight through the transom of test vessels, rather than through the bottoms of them, simply broke and kept breaking, due to the lopsided strain put on propellers that had only the bottom tips submerged.

Arneson spliced a universal joint into the shaft between the propeller and engine. The engine remained inside the boat. The universal joint was outside, covered with a flexible rubberlike housing. Arneson added hydraulic rams so the propellers could be moved around or aimed at will. Besides adding flexibility to the whole installation, this made the drives adjustable, like a stern drive. The propellers could be raised or lowered so that they just pierced the surface. They could be trimmed up or down to achieve the most efficient water/propeller interface. They could also be moved right and left, like the propeller on an outboard, for steering purposes.

Today, Arnesons are popular on high-performance boats, and twin installations have found their way into the engine rooms of some very large, very fast megayachts. Arneson boats have much less draft than conventionally driven ones, since the transom-mounted propellers and running gear are not under the hull but close to the surface of the water, even when maneuvering at slow speeds.

I've run a few Arneson boats at high speed. They were maneuverable, fun to drive. It was easy to forget the boats were Arnesons, until, that is, we got back to the dock. Maneuvering an Arneson-driven boat in close quarters takes some getting used to. I would recommend that a first-time buyer of an Arneson-driven boat get some instruction before attempting to maneuver his purchase around a dock.

Besides the Arneson, there are other propeller-type drives that are either variations on conventional systems or on Arnesons or both. The American T-torque system and the Italian Buzzi system, for example, both derive much from the conventional inboard while rearranging its components. The Liaan drive does the same thing, but more radically.

As we've already discovered, water jets are not new. In principle they operate much like jet engines in airplanes. Water, instead of air, is admitted through an opening at the front of the unit, experiences a rise in pressure and velocity from the centrifugal action of turbinelike vanes, and is expelled through an opening at the rear of the unit to provide thrust.

The jet concept has been applied to both inboard and outboard systems, with plenty of goodwill but little success. Large units on megayachts are quite common today, but it's the recent proliferation of the much smaller, snowmobilelike personal water vehicles (PWVs) that's enticing the wacky water jet out of the closet. Because of the PWV craze, there are probably more water jets being built today than ever before in history. PWVs combine the handling characteristics of motorcycles with the slipperiness of waterskis.

One of the latest innovations in the field of marine propulsion is the application of rotary engines to conventional inboard and stern-drive configurations. One engine company is offering a Japanese rotary engine teamed up with an American-built jet drive.

Surfacing drives, although a little esoteric and expensive even today, are highly efficient. They impart thrust without sacrificing speed to the drag inherent in underwater propellers.

The advantages of the rotary engine are smooth operation and reduction in size and weight. Right now, the disadvantage is cost. Whether the rotary will ever gain acceptance in the motorboating mainstream is hard to say. Certainly, if the rotary becomes popular enough, prices may come down.

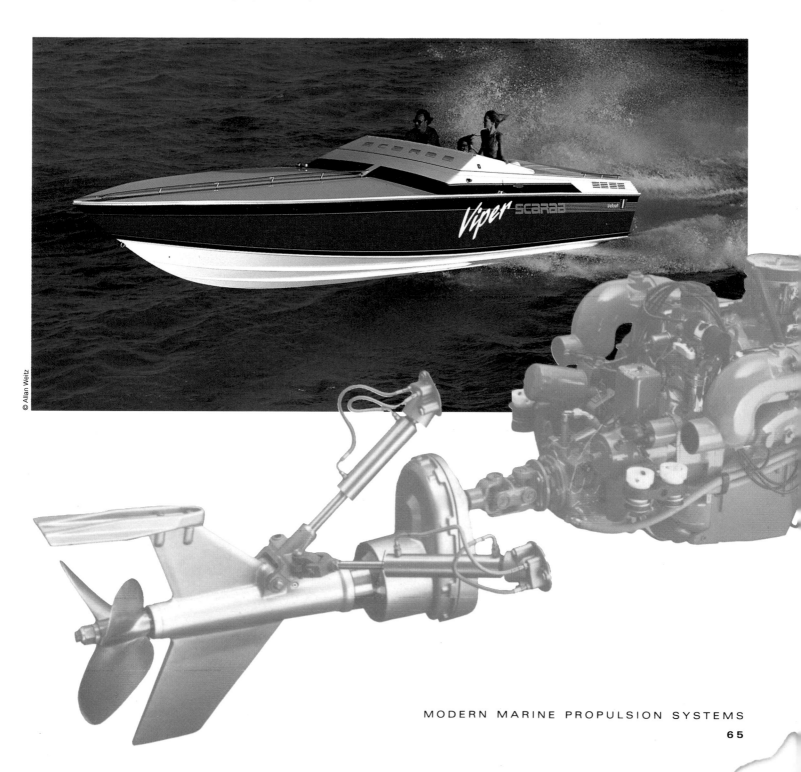

© Allan Weitz

MODERN MARINE PROPULSION SYSTEMS

BUYING YOUR BOAT

© Allan Weitz

William Atkin once advised that it was a lot easier to buy a boat than to sell one. Atkin was no armchair yachtsman; he designed both motor- and sailboats during the early part of this century, made all sorts of voyages in each type, and wrote for the boating magazines. Atkin delivered his advice tongue only partly in cheek.

For most people, the purchase of a boat, particularly if it's a big, full-displacement type, such as a fifty-foot (15-m) Hatteras Convertible, represents the largest cash outlay of their lives, except maybe their homes and funerals.

This was certainly true for me when I bought *Misty* in Gulfport, Florida, and began living aboard. That lovely old boat cost me a small fortune, which, it just so happened, was a little larger than the fortune I was subsisting on at the time.

Misty was worth every penny. She became my home and sanctuary, in fact, my single most valuable possession. Purchasing her was relatively easy. It was simply a matter of paying more money than I could conceivably pay back in one lifetime. A staunch believer in reincarnation, I paid without blinking an eye.

When it came time to sell *Misty*, despite the beauty, even elegance, I perceived in her, customers were few and far between. *Misty* was a "character" boat, which simply means that she was a little odd. A little idiosyncratic. It took months to find an oddball who saw her true character.

Atkin was right, and he was also right when he said that it's often as tough to sell a boat without character as it is to sell a boat with character.

Sensory overload. Given the variety out there, if you can't find your boat at a modern boat show, you probably need to look again.

CAVEAT EMPTOR

One major point to remember when you're buying a boat, new or used, is this: The boatbuyer has (or should have) the upper hand. Don't think that just because you're interested in a particular boat, everybody else is, too. Whether the boat is sitting proudly in some expensive showroom, or sitting in somebody's backyard, it more than likely will continue to sit for at least a few more days unless, of course, there are hundreds of people queued up at the transom waving their checkbooks.

Another major point to keep in mind is this: Approach all boatsellers with some skepticism. Even if the seller is a friend, you can be sure that the prospect of selling a boat may make him a little eager.

Some professional boat salespeople are even less trustworthy than the amateurs. Certainly, it's unfair and discriminatory to bad-mouth boat salespeople as a group, as many of them are knowledgeable and experienced individuals. Unfortunately, there are a few who are not so fine. Don't be taken in by their theatrics.

Here's a common trick some boat salespeople may use: You, the hapless customer, are sitting in the showroom. You want to buy a trailerable boat, but there are a few features that are bothering you. One of them is the trailer. You think it should be included in the deal, free of charge.

The salesperson's response to this is mildly incredulous. His boss would look upon such a proposal as a sure sign of schizophrenia. Eventually, you persuade him to call the boss. With apparent misgiving, he does so in your presence, and has a big argument about giving you the trailer for free. Finally, the boss gives in. But it was close.

So now, you're really hooked, even though there are some other aspects of the deal you're not too keen about. It appears that the salesperson has gone way out on a limb, even risked his job, to get you the deal you require. How can you possibly not buy the boat he wants you to buy? You start digging for your wallet.

The world is full of motorboats on trailers with FOR SALE signs on them.

© Christopher Bain

What's the scam? The trailer (or the VHF radio, or the extra battery, or the compass, etc.) was free to begin with. Before you ever walked into the dealership, the salesperson and his boss had agreed to pare down the standard equipment list a bit, so that you, the customer, could be offered some "real deals."

The salesperson wasn't calling the boss on the telephone, but the boss's secretary or the weather report or his mother. All the ranting and raving? As I said, pure theater.

As if the boat dealership salespeople weren't enough to contend with, you'll need to beware of the boat show charmers, too.

I remember the first boat show I ever went to. It was a high-and-dry affair in Syracuse, New York, and to a neophyte like me, it appeared to be peopled with descendants of Neptune himself. I can remember traipsing around star struck, daunted by the proliferation of boat shoes, Greek fisherman's hats, and boating jargon. I was afraid to approach a salesperson or anyone else, for that matter. Tanned people wearing blue blazers frightened me most, especially if they were standing in front of what I imagined were full-blown thirty-foot (9-m) yachts. Everybody looked so darn nautical.

Luckily, most of my discretionary income at the time had been eaten up by my pilgrimage from the hinterlands to the big city. I suppose that had I had the money to even consider buying a boat at the show, and the courage to actually write a check, I'd have bought one of the boats from the salesman with the gold chain around his neck and a beard like the one Gregory Peck sported in his role as Ahab in *Moby Dick*. This would have proven quite disastrous, I might add, since the old gent had me darn near convinced that the twenty-two-footers (6.6 m) he was selling were veritable ocean cruisers, capable of doubling Cape Horn. I don't think he was being dishonest about the whole thing. He was simply doing the best job he could, handicapped as he was, with a very lethal combination: a limited knowledge of boats but a hearty appreciation of them nevertheless, all mixed up with a very salty appearance.

Don't buy just any old boat. Make sure your choice works for the area you'll be using it in. Otherwise, a peaceful weekend may turn into a purgatorial episode.

What I'm getting at is this: Some salespeople look informed and knowledge-able, even saltily so, but they're not. Backed up with the right clothes, an exotic accent of some sort, and a spiel that's been thoroughly committed to memory, essentially lubberly and unknowledgeable salespeople can be more convinc-ing than the prophets of old. Why? Because they are basically sincere.

Watch out for insincere boat salespeople, too. They're usually in a hurry. They're a swashbuckling version of the true-believing telemarketer who uses a crib sheet to unimaginatively sell you a magazine subscription you don't want. They're usually dumb and will try to make you feel dumb, too.

Con artists are not confined to the small-boat marketplace, either. The world of megayachts has a few, their only qualifications being a loose liaison with a stable of vessels and a larcenous heart. They'd sell their mothers to the glue factory and call it a good day's work.

So once you've developed enough healthy skepticism to survive in the marine marketplace, what do you do next?

Take a tip from the Boy Scouts. Be Prepared. Long before you start talking with boatsellers about boats, you should have enough self-awareness to know whether you're serious about buying. It's not fair to the salesperson, yourself, or anyone else you habitually drag along on shopping safaris to wander from one dealership to the next grandly promising to buy when you really won't or can't.

So, before you actually start looking around, make up your mind whether you want and can afford a new model. Or will a used one do just as nicely? You should have a good idea what kind of vessel you're looking for, where you expect to use it, and under what type of conditions. You should have taken a realistic look at the state of your finances and what you can really afford. Don't forget to consider extra costs such as insurance, outfitting, safety equipment, electronics, and storage. Last but most certainly not least, you should have a good idea about how to quickly spot a well-built boat and how to spot a poorly built one, so you don't waste a lot of time hanging around with mongrels when you should be associating with greyhounds.

In the following pages, we're going to look at the best way to buy a boat. Once you've learned the techniques and developed good instinctive responses, then, *and only then,* should you head for a boat show, a showroom floor, or wherever else there's a boat with a FOR SALE sign on it.

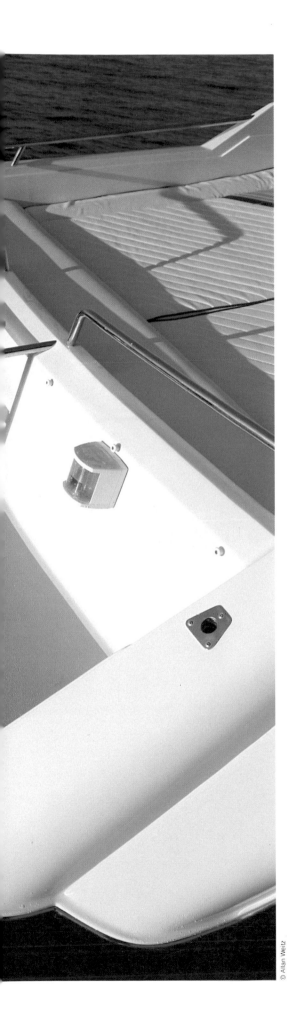

THE FEVER STRIKES

Unlike most maladies, boat-buying fever is a thoroughly pleasant affliction. It's very much like being on the verge of falling in love with any number of different people. And as with any other lover, a person who is afflicted with "The Fever" usually becomes a bit, well, imbalanced, especially if he's new to the game.

To protect themselves from unscrupulous or overzealous boat salespeople, boatbuyers must learn to immediately recognize the symptoms of "The Fever" when it strikes. It makes no difference whether you're an old hand at the game or brand new. To wander blithely through the marine marketplace, afflicted but unaware, is to tempt fate. Rather than "Born to Cruise," the theme song for your nautical endeavors may become "Born to Lose."

Here are the symptoms to look for:

1) Loss of control while driving your automobile in the vicinity of marinas, boat yards, or any other place where boats are kept. It won't matter whether your spouse and kids are in the car or not. "The Fever" simply elicits irresponsible behavior. It's not unusual for a person who's in the market for a new (or used) boat to be driving along at a good clip with both hands on the wheel, while, at the very same time he or she is staring out the back window of the car.

2) A proliferation of boating magazines and manufacturers' brochures. Stacks of them. In the bathroom, on the coffee table, by the bed, in the car (for checking details while driving past marinas and boat yards), and (why not be as honest about this whole thing as possible) in your desk at work.

3) Fixation upon the topic of boats. Once "The Fever" has got you, unless a conversation is boat related, it just doesn't seem worthwhile. This is particularly hard on loved ones and bosses, who would rather talk about other subjects sometimes. Thought patterns also suffer. The old stream of consciousness gets overrun with runabouts and trawlers, or whatever kind of vessel you're in the market for. Boat dreams are common, too.

4) Secret calculator punching. Whenever you find yourself sitting in your office, stealthily stealing a few minutes from your employer, using a calculator to test the feasibility of marine-related financial schemes, know for sure that "The Fever" is working on you. With a little prodding, you may be capable of taking out a third mortgage on the house, selling the dog, or forcing your two-year-old to get a job. Clandestine calculation may also occur in the bathroom. Or bedroom. On buses or trains or planes. Even while you drive past marinas and boat yards, with the spouse and kids screaming at you to keep your eyes on the road.

When inspecting a potential purchase, the boatbuyer must pay attention to everything, from the layout of the steering console (left) and of the swim platform (center), to the quality of the deck hardware (right)

NEW, USED, OR OTHERWISE?

Once you've determined, through a certain amount of self-observation (which is often painful), that you have "The Fever," don't get rattled. Instead, sit back and relax. Take a deep breath. Accept your pleasant little malady. Essentially, you are a lover now, surrounded by potential beloveds.

This is a wonderful situation, actually. But the field must be narrowed down, or you're going to lose your mind.

Start by asking yourself whether you want to buy a new or a used boat. Both types have advantages and disadvantages. Personally, I'm a used-boat advocate. I can't see paying top dollar for any vehicle, whether boat or otherwise, when I know I'm going to lose money through depreciation as soon as I sign on the dotted line. But there are a lot of other reasons besides money that put me on the side of the used boat.

First, the selection of used boats out there is excellent, maybe better than the selection of new ones. In some categories, such as full-displacement hulls, the selection of used boats is most assuredly better than new ones. This is simply because manufacturers these days tend to emphasize semi-displacement and planing hulls. But while planers and semiplaners are decidedly faster than the old-fashioned displacement boats, they are usually not as efficient, a point that is becoming increasingly important, as more and more people wake up to the fact that the world's oil reserves are not inexhaustible.

Why is such a variety of used boats available today? The question can be answered in one word: fiberglass. Boat building changed radically with the dawn of fiberglass in the late 1950s, and consequently, so did the market for used and new boats.

When wood was replaced by plastic as *the* boat-building material, boats ceased being biodegradable. This was a revolutionary development. Boats had always been subject to decomposition, the speed of which was indirectly proportional to the amount of time the owner devoted to maintenance. Even when boats were made of alternative building materials such as aluminum, steel, or reinforced concrete, none of which have ever caught on with mainstream buyers, they could disintegrate rather quickly if you didn't keep an eye on them.

The perils of wooden-boat ownership are legion. Wood is subject to the invasion of bugs, worms, and rot. The repair of a wooden boat's hull can often lead to complexities seemingly equaled only on the operating table. Maintenance on a comparatively small, twenty-six-foot (7.8-m) wooden boat can turn into a full-time job. I know from experience. You wind up continually working on the boat and never actually using it.

Although some people much prefer the ride, looks, and even the smell of a wooden boat, they must admit that the modern fiberglass boat is vastly superior to it in several important respects: fiberglass is cheaper; it is easier to work with; but most important of all, it is, as far as anyone knows, virtually indestructible.

There are more new boats on the market today than ever before. Whether you want a sporty, modern-looking model (opposite, top) or a model reminiscent of earlier times (opposite, bottom), you should be able to find a boat that is just right for you.

Certainly, the invention of fiberglass has exponentially increased the number of *old* boats in the world. Granted, not all of them are great buys. Poor manufacturing techniques, which we'll talk about later on, have produced some blistered fiberglass lemons that are rotting hulks today. But many old boats, built by conscientious companies as long ago as the early 1960s, can look and be as good as new boats when given a paint job.

Another advantage of the used boat is that it's probably already pretty well outfitted with electronics and safety equipment. You don't have to add a lot of extras to the purchase price. Moreover, you don't have to spend hours installing equipment and antennas, or paying others to do it. The gear's already installed and, what's more, already works.

Which brings us to the last advantage of the used boat. If it's been properly outfitted and cared for, it usually is not prone to bugs and glitches. If it's in reasonably good shape, a used boat's systems should function properly, without the many service calls over minor matters that will probably plague a new-boat buyer.

Still, to some buyers, used boats, or pre-owned boats, as the modern euphemism has it, just don't make the grade. These buyers want a new boat with that new-boat aroma, a compound of the smells of fresh fiberglass, fresh upholstery, and fresh wood. To them, there is nothing quite like owning something nobody's owned before.

Then there's the matter of equipping a new boat, with electronics, safety equipment, and accessories. Some people really enjoy this. They look upon a new boat as a clean slate and an excellent opportunity to relocate, redesign, or improve a particular installation, based on knowledge gleaned from the operation of former boats.

(We'll discuss insurance more fully later. For the time being, however, it will suffice to say that it's often difficult to insure a really old boat, or one built of wood, or any of the alternative materials mentioned earlier. And usually, where insurance people dare not enter, loan officers of banks fear to tread.)

Here's an advantage to buying a new boat, although it's a little esoteric, pertaining, as it does, to the high-rise end of the boat-buying hierarchy. The purchase of a new boat, especially a large and complex one, may be preceded by a building process in which the boat owner becomes involved. Big boat builders, like Hatteras, for example, customize their boats, at least to some extent, and solicit guidance from customers on many phases of construction, from layout to interior design. Hatteras, in fact, maintains spare offices and other facilities at its big boat-building facilities, so owners can continue to transact business as they live nearby and take part in the building process.

Finally, are there other ways to acquire a boat? Are there categories other than "new" and "used"? Yes. You can build small boats, either of wood or fiberglass, at home by using plans and materials from boat-kit manufacturers or by purchasing materials locally and using store-bought plans or plans excerpted from boating magazines.

© Allan Weitz

Just because a boat is used doesn't mean it has to look that way. Old boats, once cleaned, repaired, and polished, can look better than they did the day they were launched.

I once read about a couple of men who built a wooden boat, from a kit that arrived in several manageably sized boxes, in a twentieth-floor apartment. Of course, once the contents of the boxes were assembled, they had a problem. Eventually, they were constrained to saw this boat in half to get it into the elevator. Once the two halves were reassembled and fiberglassed together, the boat was as good as new.

So don't despair if you live in a cramped apartment. Build the boat somewhere and then figure out how to get it to the water. A word of warning: I've built a few boats in basements and can testify that the completion of any given project invariably takes longer than predicted.

You can also build your own boat, from scratch, without plans. I did it once, in my youth. Based on that experience, I wouldn't recommend it. The creation of a full-blown vessel from scratch, particularly by an amateur, leaves a little too much elbowroom for creativity.

Restoring or refurbishing an old boat has many advantages. One of the most important ones, as superbly illustrated here, has to do with the beauty and distinctive look of wood.

© Marty Loken/Allstock

The strangest vessel of the from-scratch variety I've ever seen was built over a period of about ten years, without much in the way of plans, by a retired gentleman living in the Deep South. He built the sixty-footer (18 m) in his backyard and had it trucked to the water. The boat was constructed entirely from materials he'd been able to buy at local hardware stores, with not a single marine-grade component.

To the casual observer, standing at a distance, the boat looked sort of like a megayacht, especially just after her smart coat of house paint had been refreshed. But up close, the thing looked like a heinous head-on collision between a tract house and all the evil spirits of naval architecture.

Little scrutiny was required to tell that her hull was made of sheets of plain plywood, held together with construction adhesive and nails. I seriously doubt that this craft still floats after the passage of these several years. For her builder's sake, I hope she went down in shallow water. And I hope the adjustable recliner in the cockpit, with the flowery upholstery, went down with her.

A boat's name is most commonly displayed on the transom. Once you buy a boat, it is considered bad luck to change its name.

SELECTING THE BOAT YOU WANT TO BUY

Once you've got the new, used, or otherwise question solved, ask yourself another question. What kind of boat do you want to buy? By this, I don't mean asking yourself whether you want to buy a sportfisherman, or a runabout, or a ski boat. I assume you already know what you want to do with your vessel.

Once you've decided you're interested in a runabout or a small cruiser, for example, then you have to decide what kind of runabout or small cruiser you actually want to buy.

The best way to approach this question is to look realistically at your boating experience, where and under what conditions you expect to use the boat, and where you expect to keep it. This last consideration is very important, and we'll discuss it at the end of this chapter.

To begin with, think about size. Ideally, a boatman gets experience in smaller boats before he buys bigger ones. This approach is old-fashioned, but it is very sensible. It will prevent embarrassment as well as damage and the financial and other heartaches that damage can sometimes bring.

When buying a boat, don't get carried away. If you already own a small cruiser, the perfect new boat should be only a couple of feet longer, no more. Besides being more comfortable, this new size will challenge your handling skills, but not excessively. A motorboating friend of mine bought a new boat and made a jump of almost ten feet (3 m) in waterline length. This was a mistake. After buying the new boat, he seldom used it, primarily because he was afraid to dock and undock it.

Next, before you buy a particular kind of boat, have a good idea of what sort of sea conditions you expect to use it in. Will you keep the boat on a freshwater lake where a one-foot (30-cm) chop is the worst you'll have to deal with? Will you run shallow rivers with dangerous sandbars that guard them from the sea? Will you fish in turbulent waters or cruise long distances in calm waters? Pick the boat that best suits the weather and other conditions of your home waters.

For example, a small fishing boat with a hard top is fine for a northern lake. There, an enclosure of roof and windows makes a lot of sense, especially when the temperature starts to drop. But in tropical waters, a center-console-type boat, with a collapsible bimini or T-Top for shade, will probably work better. It will give you better fuel economy (less wind resistance) and, since the boat is not all cluttered up with an enclosure, more fish-fighting elbowroom.

Regardless of what a salesperson may tell you, boats are built with different venues in mind. Some people dream of ocean voyaging, for example, and have little idea of what this means. Consequently, they are under the impression that all they need is a big boat. Wrong. Even most full-displacement cruisers and big semidisplacement sportfishermen must be modified for serious offshore tripping.

First determine how you will use your boat, then take out your checkbook. Why buy a family cruiser when what you really want is a ski boat?

courtesy OMC

Realistically, the majority of mainstream production boats built today are coastal boats at best. While they may be capable of island hopping, I can think of very few models that are beefy enough and have enough watertight integrity fresh from the factory to cross an open ocean safely.

Some people want nothing to do with the ocean, preferring to cruise inland rivers and lakes. This is a lovely way to travel; it's like living on a moving cottage. You can cruise a river in vessels that are much less beefy and seaworthy than those designed for offshore or coastal cruising. It makes little sense for a buyer interested in living aboard and cruising a peaceful river to spend a lot of extra money on a blue-water cruiser with a thick hull of solid glass, watertight bulkheads, armor-plate windows, and humongous diesel engines when a low-horsepower, low-priced houseboat will do.

Finally, before you buy a boat, try to get to know somebody who owns one, particularly one like the model you're hankering to buy. Boatmen worth their salt love to talk about their boats.

Find out if the owner is satisfied with the kind of boat he owns. Is the engine powerful enough? Does the boat track well? Does the boat produce an inordinate wake? Is there some other brand or type of boat he would like to buy?

By cultivating knowledgeable acquaintances, you can learn a great deal about the kind of boat you want before you go shopping. Another good thing to do is read boating magazines. By doing this, you'll get a good idea of what kinds of boats may exist in your chosen category. If you've got a favorite magazine, try calling up one of the editors. He may prove helpful, although, more than likely, he will avoid the endorsement of a particular manufacturer.

Quality differs. Whether it's joinery, the relative heft of deck fittings, or the ease with which the engine controls (below) can be operated, remember that you usually get what you pay for.

© Allan Weitz

MASTER OF ALL YOU SURVEY

Before buying any boat, survey it yourself or have it surveyed by a competent professional. What's a survey? The term simply means an accurate appraisal of the worth of a vessel, based on a closer inspection of its construction, equipment, and state of repair. Obviously, surveying is a must for used boats. Few banks will make a loan on a used boat unless it has been approved by a reputable surveyor, and getting insurance on a used boat without a survey is just about unheard of.

Most new boats are a different matter. Professional surveyors are seldom employed, which means it's more or less up to the buyer to determine the quality of the vessel. Following is a checklist of what you should look for, and look out for, when surveying your potential purchase.

I'm not saying that once you've armed yourself with an understanding of this list you can jump right into the business of professional surveying, although there are some people in the field who started out with less. But hopefully the list will help you to separate the wheat from the chaff. We're going to stick to fiberglass boats here, because they're the most common. Used with common sense, this list should work for boats that are either new or used.

AN AMATEUR MARINE SURVEYOR'S CHECKLIST

1) Stand at the stern of the boat you're interested in and look forward along the hull sides. Adjust your position, looking for dimples, ripples, and anything inconsistent with a smooth, even surface. Irregularities can't be covered up with gel coat (the outer cosmetic covering of the fiberglass), and indicate either that the mold used to make the boat was imperfect or worn out. Imperfections may also indicate that the hull wasn't given enough time to cure in the mold, or that excess resin was not squeezed out of the laminate as it was laid up in the mold. The latter causes "hot spots," or places where the glass pulls away from the mold because of heat-activated expansion during the curing process.

Whatever the reason for their existence, irregularities in the surface of the fiberglass are not good. They indicate poor quality, even though they would seem to create no difficulties other than cosmetic ones. They point to sloppy lay-up processes that can cause delamination and other structural problems a few years down the road.

2) Now get up close to the hull. Again, adjust your position and look for woven pattern of glass fabric in the hull. The pattern usually has the consistency you'd associate with a burlap bag. If you're looking at a good boat, you should see no pattern at all.

There are a number of reasons why the pattern of the fiberglass cloth used to construct the hull of a boat may show through. The most obvious is that the gel coat is too thin. Ideally, gel coat should be about twenty-two millimeters thick. If the gel is thicker, it is likely to be brittle and crack.

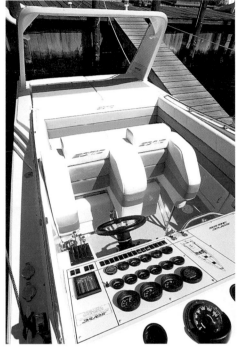

One of the best ways to tell whether a boat is right for you is simply to use a little common sense. Sit down in the driver's seat. Do you feel comfortable? Can you see through the windshield? Can you see the instruments? Do the throttles slide smoothly? What about the shifts? After all, boats are machines. They should work smoothly.

Here's a quick way to test the bridge ladder: grip it with both hands and shake it. A good ladder is virtually immovable.

In addition to making the boat look bad, skimping on the gel coat can cause other problems. When left to its own devices, fiberglass absorbs water like a slow-motion sponge. Besides making a boat look pretty, gel coat acts as a barrier and helps keep out the water. When applied too thinly, gel coat can't do its job.

A word of warning: If there's no apparent pattern, or "print-through," in a hull, that doesn't guarantee the gel-coat job is adequate. Often, in the laminating process, companies add a layer of short glass strands and resin—a totally random application—between the gel coat and the first layer of fiberglass cloth to prevent any sort of organized pattern from showing through.

So study a patch or patches of the hull on any prospective purchase. If you detect anything but a smooth, fair surface, the gel coat may be inadequate. You now have a right to suspect that other things about this particular boat may not be all they're cracked up to be.

3) Look around the interior of the boat. Most fiberglass vessels are composed of three parts: hull, deck, and liner. These three parts should all fit together tightly, with no wide cracks or crevices between.

Avoid boats with cracks. Avoid boats with a lot of wood or plastic molding and trim pieces covering cracks. Trim and molding camouflage of this sort is especially noticeable in the cockpit, where cracks can't be hidden with fabric and upholstery like they can be below deck. The more trim there is in the cockpit, the less faith you should have in the salesperson's claim that the boat just recently made a spectacularly long passage. Excess trim means that you, as an owner, are going to suffer, from both the standpoint of maintenance and from the standpoint of durability and strength.

With time, boats composed of numerous loose-fitting pieces shake themselves apart due to the vibration inherent in running over or through the water. They're not as strong as other apparently simpler but in fact much more complex boats. More pieces means less structural integrity. Boats like this also squeak, groan, and grate in any type of a seaway. This may seem like a small point, but it will take on new significance when your passengers become terrified enough from the racket to threaten mutiny.

Why do some manufacturers build their boats in many pieces? Money. The creation of molds, or "tooling," with many aspects of design built in is a complex, time-consuming, and expensive job. It's much easier to put in a set of cockpit steps as a separate entity, for example, than to mold it into the liner.

4) Ask the salesperson, or whoever is showing you around the boat, exactly how the hull and the deck are put together. A good joint is a strong indicator of strength and quality. Most hulls and decks fit together like a shoe box and its lid. The best type of joint is made as follows:

A waterproof marine sealant is laid on between the overlapping flanges of the deck and hull. Holes are drilled on six- to eight-inch (15- to 20-cm) centers through the flanges, around the gunwale of the boat. Then bolts are run through the holes from outside. The bolts are backed up with large fender washers and aviation-type locknuts. The joint is then glassed over from inside the boat, effectively bonding hull and deck into one single piece. Finally, an aluminum or stainless-steel extrusion is fitted along the outside of the joint and secured with screws at intervals that fall midway between the countersunk heads of the bolts. The extrusion contains a band of hard rubber to absorb the shock of docking.

The least agreeable joint leaves out the sealant and the part where the joint inside the boat is glassed over. Screws, plain and simple, will be substituted for the bolts, washers, and locknuts. Sometimes builders anchor the screws in an interior strip of wood, but sometimes they don't.

If the salesperson doesn't seem to know about the hull-to-deck joint, he should. And he should also not mind if you go poking around in a locker or two, trying to see the joint. There's usually someplace aboard every boat where you can get a look at it.

5) Now it's time to take a look at the engine room, and more particularly, the engine mounts, which hold the engine in place and keep it from spinning like the cylinder of a revolver due to the torque developed in the drive train.

The trend used to be, even in some fairly sizable boats, to use lag screws to secure the engine to the bottom of the boat, or more accurately, to the longitudinal strengtheners at the bottom of the boat. The strengtheners, since they are commonly made of fiberglass and cored with plywood or thick softwood planks, would hold the screws securely.

While the lag-bolt arrangement may be adequate for smaller boats, like runabouts and small cruisers, it doesn't make sense for larger ones. Vibration in big engines is wont to loosen the lag screws. Proper engine mounts, usually short pieces of aluminum or steel angle, work much better. Ordinarily, one flange is bolted through the side of a longitudinal strengthener or stringer (with backing plate, washer, and aviation-type locknut), and the other flange supports one "corner" of the engine itself.

What else should you look for in the engine room? The orderly layout of the electrical and plumbing systems is a good barometer of quality. An engine room festooned with mazes of seemingly unidentified wires and pipes means troubleshooting and repairs will be nightmarish, and probably indicates the existence of shoddy workmanship elsewhere in the boat.

6) Once you've finished going through the engine room, sit down in some comfortable spot aboard and start fantasizing. Imagine how you're going to use this boat, or how your family is going to use it. Where are the children going to sleep? Where are you going to sleep? Are things arranged sensibly? Do you have to discombobulate the dinette table to get into the head? Is there plenty of ventilation? Or is the midcabin an airless, dark fiberglass cave? At the helm, can you see where you're going, both sitting down and standing up? Are the mattresses in the berths thick and long enough to sleep on? Can you get at the dipsticks and oil fills on the engines? All of these things are important.

Sit down in the dinette/galley area, and ask yourself some practical, spending-the-night-on-the-boat questions. Does the stove have one burner or two? Is the refrigerator big enough? Can you wash a plate in the sink?

© Darrell Jones

While you're fantasizing, try to recall the other boats you've looked at. How does this one compare, in terms of finish? Do pieces fit? Is the joiner work mediocre or is it cabinet quality? Are the upholstered seats well finished, or are there raw edges of fabric and fiberglass underneath? Is the bilge gel-coated? Or is it simply painted or left raw, to absorb water? Do things look solid? Or do they look like they might fall apart shortly?

7) Last but not least. I have twice purchased boats without sea trialing. In both cases, I was lucky. Each boat turned out fine. So the following advice falls into the do-as-I-say-not-as-I-do category. There are plenty of motorboatmen who were not so lucky.

Sea-trial the boat before you buy it. Find out how the vessel performs, hands on. Sure, you may get lucky. But it's best not to rely solely on the vagaries of good fortune to protect you when buying a boat. You might just as well try docking a tug in a forty-knot crosswind by simply hoping for the best. Things work out so much better if you actually do something.

Whether the salesperson or owner allows you to handle the boat around the dock is up to him. Frankly, I wouldn't push it. Who knows? You may be dealing with a person who subscribes to the apothegm, "You break it...you bought it."

Once you're in open water, ask to drive the boat. See how it steers. Does it "pull" to the right or left due to propeller torque? A substantial steering bias may mean poor design. If the wind causes the boat to lay over on its side a bit, can you straighten it out easily with the trim tabs? If you can't, this is another indicator of poor design. And if your boat's a blue-water biggie, ideally you'll try her in some rough seas. How does she behave? Does she roll excessively in beam seas? Poor design again. Most boats tend to slew back and forth when running in the direction the seas are running. Make sure yours does not do so excessively.

In head seas, is there enough flare and flam in the bow to keep the spray down? There should be. If not, you are going to be continually taking water over the bow. Your boating is going to be wet and uncomfortable.

Stop the boat. Try backing it up toward a buoy or some other sizable floating object. Does she back straight? She should. Do the controls work smoothly? When you move the shifters, can you feel the detentes or spots where the engines actually go from neutral into gear and the propellers start moving? You should be able to. It's no good when the first indication that you're in gear comes when you notice the boat is moving—or when you hear a change in the engine pitch. Remember, you can't always rely on hearing to tell you whether your engines are in gear or out. The wind may be blowing hard or the stereo may be cranked full blast.

If you're a little bit shaky on all this, ask the salesperson or owner to help you. You can learn more in five minutes of hands-on experience than you can in five days of salesmanship.

INCIDENTALS THAT AREN'T SO INCIDENTAL

Once you've decided to buy a boat, you need to address a couple of very important details. Although these details have nothing to do with the boat itself, they have a lot to do with what the boat is ultimately going to cost. Depending on where you live, prices for taxes, insurance, liability coverage, hauling and storage, maintenance, and slip or mooring rentals vary. Once you know how much these things collectively cost, factor that amount into your calculations. It's better to retrench a little bit now than to find out, after buying a boat, that you don't have the means to properly care for it.

Let's talk about taxes. It used to be that boats were fairly exempt, except, of course, for sales taxes. This fact, coupled with mortgage interest deductions on boats used as second homes, was a serious booster of the boating industry in the United States.

But things are changing. User fees on most boats and luxury taxes on those costing more than $100,000 are making boating more expensive, at least in the United States.

Before you make a commitment to buy, find out from the seller how much you will have to pay in taxes. It may be more than you think.

Let's talk about insurance. I used to hate hurricane season, especially when I was a Merchant Marine officer. I spent countless nights awake in the berths of tugboats in the middle of nowhere, worrying whether some blasted hurricane was on a collision course with the far-away marina where I was keeping my boat. Eventually, I got tired of worrying and took out an insurance policy.

Ownership of large and often expensive boats usually entails some sort of financing, which, in turn, entails insurance. The only potential for grief here is that the insurance coverage may in some way be inadequate, that is, it doesn't satisfactorily cover whatever loss is incurred. There's little sense in spending a lot of money on a vessel and then trying to skimp on the insurance coverage.

Even among reputable insurance carriers, prices on policies can vary considerably. Get several quotes, from several companies that regularly insure boats, and pick the best one. Don't get mixed up with insurance people who don't know a port from a hole in the wall. Make sure your policy will cover your boat in all the areas you plan to use it. Does the policy cover coastal usage only? Or will it cover usage offshore? If so, how far offshore is it good for? How many experienced operators are required to be aboard?

As I mentioned earlier, you will discover that if you're the owner of a wood-, steel-, or aluminum-hulled vessel, insurance companies seem to be a little bit standoffish. Most, in fact, will simply refuse to have anything to do with a wooden boat. Prior to writing a policy on any sort of big metal boat, most companies will require that every single square foot of the hull be checked for thickness with an audio gauge, a procedure that is very expensive and must be repeated periodically.

Today, megayachts (opposite) are more expensive to own than ever before, primarily because of luxury taxes and increases in costs related to ownership, such as insurance, dockage, and maintenance.

In addition to insuring the boat itself against damage, you should think about liability coverage. Get a lot of liability insurance, at least enough to cover your net worth, which you could need in the event of a serious accident. Look at it this way. This is one of the few times that it's really advantageous to be poor.

Except on new boats, insurance companies will usually require a survey prior to issuing a policy. If a company offers to write a policy without a survey, a red flag should go up in your mind. The company is probably not reputable.

© Neil Rabinowitz

Taking care of business often means managing your fun while managing other things at the same time, like slip rent and liability coverage.

While insurance is imperative on big boats, it is not as important to small-boat owners. Most of my recreational boating has been done aboard small boats, without insurance. Luckily, I enjoyed myself and suffered no ill effects... knock on wood.

While we're on the subject of incidental costs, unless you've bought a trailerable motorboat or own property that adjoins the water, keeping your boat somewhere is going to cost you money. How much it will cost depends on where you live and how exalted your tastes are. Before you buy a boat, check with some local boat yards and marinas. Find out how much a slip will cost. Do some comparison shopping. Most places charge by the foot. Small is definitely better when you're looking to rent a slip.

Another option is the mooring. If you decide to go this route, make sure that the marina offering the moorings also offers a competent and timely launch service. If they don't, make sure they don't charge an arm and a leg to store your dinghy, to get to the mooring.

There will be other costs involved. If your boat is fairly large, you'll have to pay to have it hauled out of the water so that you can store it over the winter or perhaps do some maintenance, such as the renewal of its antifouling bottom paint. Then, after the winter, or the bottom job, you'll have to pay to have the boat returned to the water.

It's also a good idea to find a boat yard you can trust. I love boat yards, especially the kind with an ambience of dilapidation. Sadly, the real boat yards, the ones that smell of paint, gasoline, and gunk, the ones that are inhabited by crazy pipe-smoking old coots wearing paint-spattered jeans, are being replaced by sterile marinas and marina/condominium complexes.

It's too bad. Boat yards are wonderful places to learn about boats, to buy boats, and to get cut-rate services for boats. Sometimes, if you hit the right boat-yard owner with just the right tale of woe, he'll do you a deal that approximates a miracle.

The ideal boat yard is a little offbeat. Situated in an out-of-the-way spot, it will haul your boat, or provide other services for about half the going rate. You've got to hunt out places like these. You've also got to be careful when you think you've found one. The equipment may be questionable, particularly the heavy machinery. It's a good idea to be at the yard when anything important is going on, such as lifting your boat from the briny.

All dilapidated boat yards are not good, though. Some are staffed by maritime miscreants, every one a thief, cutthroat, or worse. Such places usually look promisingly bad, so you expect prices to be low. But prices are not. The bill comes in installments, in the mail, on the letterhead of seven savage lawyers from a distant city. How do you tell the good boat yard from the bad? For starters, look for a dog. The presence of a cheerful, lazy cur hanging about the place means you're among honest people. A bunch of dogs means you can feel safe strolling around, looking for another boat to buy.

© Christopher Bain

THE BIG MOMENT

Okay. You've decided on a boat. You've looked it over, test-driven it, and consulted with the chancellor of the exchequer on what you can expect to pay in taxes. Now it's time to write the check. But before you do, one more piece of advice. Most boat prices are negotiable. I wasted the first half of my boat-buying life needlessly depleting my cash reserves because I was unaware of this simple fact.

Many sellers of boats approach the buyer with inflated price tags. They fully expect to bargain and may even be disappointed by a buyer's lack of response. Only recently, I answered a newspaper advertisement concerning a sixteen-foot (4.8-m) boat. The initial asking price was $1,750. After only two days of amiable jockeying, the seller came down to $1,000. Granted, the time was late autumn, an ideal time to be shopping around for boats. This wild depreciation was more typical of the used, rather than the new, market.

Bargaining on boat prices is great sport. Try it, you'll like it.

Today, the public perception seems to be that motorboating is expensive. Bargain wisely, however, and who knows what kind of deal you can get on a small, used family cruiser.

A TRIP TO THE OUTFITTERS

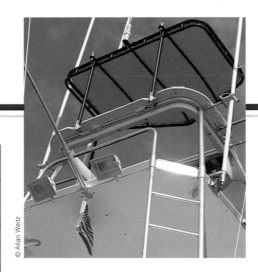

© Allan Weitz

Unless you're buying a used boat that is already very well equipped, you should have a good basic idea of how you plan to outfit a vessel before you buy it. We're not going to get into an awful lot of esoterica here. People were going to sea quite successfully long before mermaid-shaped fenders, decorative tableware, and various other nautical doodads were invented. So can you.

The reason you must decide how you want to equip your boat, previous to its purchase, is purely monetary. Before you start spending, you need to know how much all the extras are going to cost and whether you're going to have enough to pay for them.

Some boats are sold packaged, which makes everything easy. To buy such boats requires little additional money over and above the purchase price. Other boats—the majority of them, in fact—are sold at base prices with option lists that may run to several pages in length, depending on the size and complexity of the vessel.

Without a decent idea of what you absolutely need to have aboard your boat and how much all this stuff is going to cost as well, you may end up owning a brand-new motorboat and little else in the way of equipment to run her safely.

The following equipment is essential in order to assure you, your friends, and your family a minimum of comfort and safety.

Most options like electronics (opposite) and tuna towers (above) are not necessary, especially if you're talking custom installations like the ones shown here.

One secret to good service from your radio is proper antenna installation (opposite). A hand-held or portable VHF (below) makes a great auxiliary radio, either for tenders or for backup on board your boat. A hand-held's battery makes it less reliable and sometimes less powerful than a fixed set.

RADIO EQUIPMENT: VHFs AND ANTENNAS

Unless your new boat is inflatable, or a rowing shell, skiff, or dinghy, you need some sort of radio aboard. This is obviously true for big boats that venture far out on the ocean. Not only is a radio a necessity in such emergency situations as breakdowns, accidents, or injuries, it also keeps the motorboatman abreast of events in the world at large. Some of my most entertaining nights at sea have been spent listening to the world news on the single sideband.

There are basically two types of marine radios: the VHF, which just about every boat should have, and the single sideband. VHFs are by far the most common and least expensive. Single sidebands are costly, long-distance devices found on commercial and seagoing recreational watercraft. Fortunately, there are only two very simple rules to follow when buying a sideband: (1) don't buy a cheap one, and (2) have a reputable electronics technician install it for you.

Buying a VHF is a little more complicated than buying a sideband, mostly because of the proliferation of sets on the market today. You can buy VHFs for thousands of dollars that have more features than a Swiss army knife. Some VHFs will scan all channels or just the ones you preprogram, and sportfishermen can buy VHFs that visually display the bearing or compass direction to other VHF radio transmissions, so they can zero in on other fishermen who are dumb enough to blab about their catches on the air.

Some VHFs may have as many as ten weather channels, although this is rather pointless, since there are only four channels that actually carry any weather broadcasts. And VHFs come in various sizes, from hand-helds weighing only a few ounces to bigger units that can do double duty as loudhailers and foghorns.

There are more electronics companies producing VHFs today than ever before. In their separate efforts to reach a broad market, these hungry companies are emphasizing complexity, extra features, and even, Lord help us, styling. This approach is pretty silly. Who needs a high-strung and intelligent radio that's also aesthetically pleasing out there beyond the horizon? Boatmen just need VHFs that work day after day, over the long haul, under normal and emergency conditions.

The way to select a good VHF radio is to look at the essentials. Certainly, price is an important consideration, but it is not always the most important factor. I recently took a new boat cruising for a week. The boat was equipped with an expensive VHF that bore the logo of an electronics manufacturer long famous for its electronic equipment, especially radars.

We had not even left the dock when this marvel, supposedly the company's most-sophisticated-yet-simplest-to-operate VHF, began to malfunction. It could scan like you wouldn't believe; it could monitor two channels at one time; it was loaded down with extra weather and other channels just waiting for the government to decide what to do with them.

THE COMPLETE BOOK OF MOTORBOATING

But the keyboard didn't work. To get a particular channel, you had to poke away haphazardly at the unit like a punch-drunk fighter and hope for the best. Actually, this idiosyncrasy made a lot of sense in light of the way another piece of equipment, built by the same manufacturer, worked. The radar, which cost several thousand dollars, could be turned on only by pressing a button clearly marked OFF. You get the picture.

Most VHFs, except for the portable ones, have twenty-five watts of power. This makes almost every radio, no matter which manufacturer builds it, equal to every other radio, at least in its ability to send a signal. Even if a radio has more watts, its range is still going to be about fifteen to twenty miles (24 to 32 km), given the typical antenna altitude of about twenty feet (6 m). Why? VHFs send and receive signals line of sight, which means they are not effective beyond the horizon. Therefore, since physical factors limit range, the ability to transmit is not a good criteria for judging the quality of a radio, although the ability to receive certainly is.

Receptive ability can be measured in two ways: selectivity and sensitivity. A radio's selectivity is determined by how well it discriminates between the signals you want to receive and those that you don't. Sensitivity is less important, and is determined by how well the radio can pick up a weak signal and make it stand out against normal background static.

Selectivity is often expressed in negative numbers of decibels (–dB): the more negative decibels, the better the VHF's discriminating abilities (a radio with –65dB of selectivity is better than one with –60dB). The VHF's sensitivity is usually expressed as the number of microvolts (lambda V) required to produce a certain amount of signal strength; the lower the number of microvolts, the better its ability to pick up the signal. When you buy a VHF, ask the salesperson about these two qualities, and be sure to take time to look at a few units and compare them.

Another feature to evaluate is how the unit actually works. When I first went to sea, most VHFs had rotary knobs, and the channel selector was easy to read both at night and in the bright sunshine. Now many VHFs have electronic digital displays that can be difficult to read, not in the dark, but in the daytime. Ideally, you should be able to give a prospective purchase the sunlight test. Try to get the VHF outside or at least near the window, and see whether you can actually read the display in a glare.

Once you have determined that the display is readable from all angles in bright sunlight, try to get a feeling for the unit's programming. Does the radio operate logically? Does it have a separate button or switch for channel 16, the hailing and distress frequency? If not, in an emergency situation you may find yourself maniacally trying to push a couple of buttons in the right sequence. Does the radio's programming explain itself to you, the operator? Or is it hard to understand? Could you figure out how to use this radio without the manual?

Someone may try to sell you a hand-held VHF, suggesting that it makes an ideal and inexpensive substitute for a larger, more expensive model. This is not the case. Few hand-held VHFs have the full twenty-five watts of transmitting power. Most have about six, which will reduce the range of the radio to about five miles (8 km) at most, and that's with freshly charged batteries. Hand-held

Even a small boat like a single-engine family bowrider (opposite) deserves a decent radio. Without one, a minor emergency can turn into a major one.

VHFs work fine for communication between your boat and her tender or dinghy, or between your boat and a shore party, or in any other situation where long distances are not involved. But a hand-held VHF should never replace a reliable and powerful VHF at the helm. Here's why.

Many years ago I was testing a twenty-six-foot (7.8-m) center console fishing boat. Because the boat was a new model, a prototype, she'd been rushed to our test site minus her electronics package. There was no VHF. Pressed for time myself, I tossed a little hand-held VHF into the glove compartment of the boat and prepared to hit the trail. Upon casting off, I explained to a bunch of dock kibbitzers, who subsequently wandered off to a nearby bar and stayed until the joint closed, that I'd be back in less than an hour.

At the time, I didn't know that the batteries in my hand-held were close to death. Armed with a fully charged nickel cadmium battery pack, that particular radio was good for maybe six or seven hours of continuous operation. The hour or so of use that remained in my batteries was marred by a profound drop in transmitting range.

At any rate, about sunset, I ran aground, just about the time the tide was starting to recede. I had no excuse for running aground, other than that just about every other boatman has done so at one time or another. After the grounding, I sat in that twenty-six-footer (7.8 m), which sat in a pile of clam shells and mud, for a good eight hours waiting for the tide to come back and float me off. When it rained, I tried to climb into a canvas bag and sleep. The poor devil who had the distinct misfortune of accompanying me on the test tried to sleep in a fish box under a hatch in the deck.

Since the radio didn't work, and the guy who was with me was too unnerved to communicate in a civil fashion, I had to listen to myself talk. That was the real hell of it. Basically, what I was gabbing about was how I would never set foot on a boat minus a proper VHF again.

Antennas are also important. But before we begin talking about them, let me say that our antenna discussion is not going to include sideband antennas, because they are too complicated to go into here and, as I mentioned earlier, should be installed by a professional. Anyway, VHF antennas are simpler, much less expensive, and the average motorboatman is much more likely to own one.

Without a good antenna, you can own the best VHF on the market and it will not work as well as a deep, well-aimed, and resonant rebel yell. A good antenna should be many things, but primarily it should be powerful. By powerful I mean it should be capable of receiving and sending signals long distances. To ensure that the antenna can do this, try to buy one with as much gain (the measurement of an antenna's effective transmitting and receiving ability) as you can afford. Naturally, the more gain an antenna has, the more it will cost.

Make sure your antenna is physically strong. A good antenna should be as resilient as a good fly-fishing rod, but a little stiffer. Also, be aware that there's not much sense trying to mount an antenna as high as you can in your boat. Why run the risk of snapping it, when the extra couple of feet will increase your range by less than a mile? What little you gain in range may be totally lost.

The masts of most motoryachts bristle with all sorts of electronic gadgetry—radar scanners, wind speed and direction pickups, and a host of antennas, including those for loran, GPS, television, and VHF radio.

© Allan Weitz

While we're on the subject of endurance, remember that manufacturers make a lot of claims about how their products stand up to the elements. Be leery. I know of only a couple of radios that are actually waterproof. The rest are "water resistant," a term that is subject to considerable interpretation. But if a manufacturer warranties its product as waterproof, by all means give it serious consideration come purchase time.

If you do find a truly waterproof radio and buy it, don't try to drown it to prove a point. Your radio may turn out to be the most important piece of safety equipment you have on board. It should be installed in a spot where it will be well protected from the elements. If you can, install the radio in a protective fiberglass electronics box, preferably with a cover of some sort. Ideally, I would suggest having a well-protected VHF at the helm of your boat and a fully charged hand-held in the glove compartment, just in case.

Antennas should be solid— and solidly affixed to the superstructure of your boat. If they're not, whipping about in rough weather may cause them to break. A VHF with no antenna is as useful as no VHF at all.

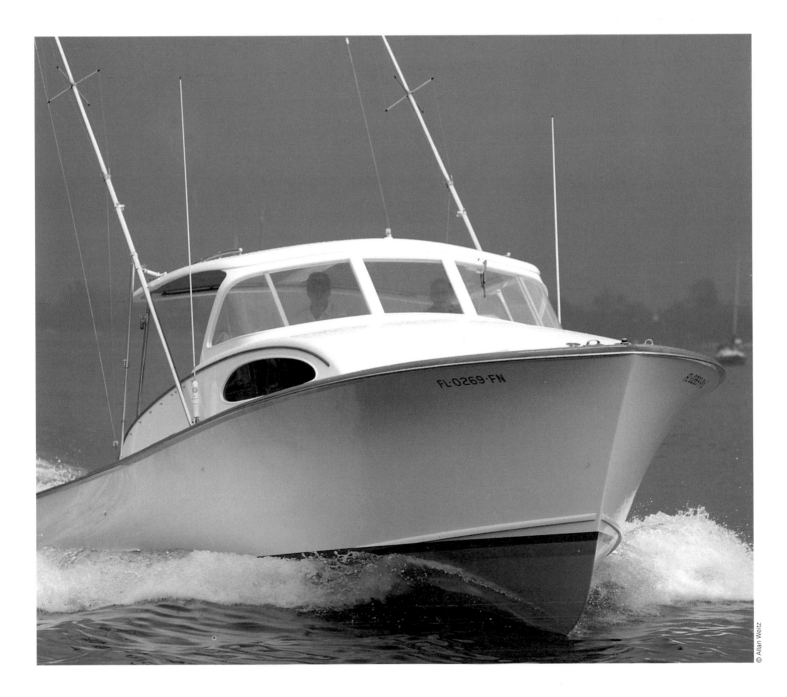

THE COMPLETE BOOK OF MOTORBOATING

© Neil Rabinowitz

COMPASSES

Before you buy a compass, an imperative piece of boating equipment, you need to know what types are available and how they differ. The magnetic compass is the most common compass. In order to understand why this old standby may need a little backup, you need to understand the two types of error the magnetic compass is subject to.

I once had a job, hauling drill pipe to oil rigs. One of the rigs I was supposed to service lay about 120 miles (192 km) offshore, in a forbidding sector of the Gulf of Mexico called the "High Island" area. The area showed no sea monsters or whirlpools on the chart, but it should have.

My first night on this particular job, just before leaving the dock, I was checking over the navigational equipment in the wheelhouse when I noticed that the magnetic compass was out of whack by a good twenty degrees. The loran, the only means of determining an exact location once we are at sea (see Electronic Navigational Devices, this chapter), didn't work, either.

The vessel I'd been assigned to was an oldie, but not so goldie, called the *Point Conception.* Those who knew her well, I was to learn later on, called her the *Point Contraption.*

The marine superintendent of the company I worked for at the time was on board helping the chief engineer deal with some major mechanical problems. All mechanical problems were major aboard the *Conception,* it would turn out. Once the superintendent had assured himself that the engines would at least make it to the rig, he strolled up to the bridge to see how things were going among the fox hunters.

On the water, steering by compass is about the most time-honored way of maintaining a straight course (opposite), although there are other ways to do so. Today's lorans, for example, have directional abilities. But a compass, like the one here (above), is more reliable in the long run.

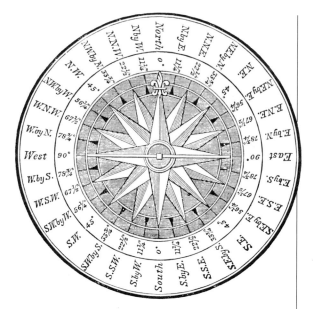

Fig. 1.—Compass Card.

The compass rose brings to mind an exercise that's taught at maritime academies: "boxing the compass." The exercise involves the memorization and subsequent chanting of all thirty-two points of the compass (shown here). Unfortunately, being able to do this will be of absolutely no use to you.

"How am I going to travel 120 miles (192 km) in the dark and hit an oil rig in the middle of nowhere right on the nose without a loran or a compass?" I asked him.

"Well," he drawled, "Magellan did it."

Technically, this wasn't quite true, of course. But the old Portuguese navigator did not have 90,000 tons (81,000 metric t) of drill pipe on his back deck like I did. That pipe was causing a magnificent example of magnetic compass error known in the trade as deviation.

Deviation will throw any magnetic compass off. It can be caused by the presence of metal, such as drill pipe, in the vicinity of a compass, or by electronics or electrical wiring, or even repairs effected through welding aboard steel vessels. Worse, deviation varies with the course a vessel may steer.

The only way to figure out how much your compass is deviating is to actually measure it. This is a pain in the neck, and entails swinging your boat through 360 degrees, comparing known bearings on ranges ashore with the bearings your compass gives you, to create a deviation table with a reading for every fifteen degrees.

In the oil field you do not have a lot of spare time. You certainly don't have the leisure to swing ship every time you take on a new load of drill pipe.

The second type of magnetic-compass error is variation, and is a little more predictable. Variation results from the discrepancy between the earth's geographic and magnetic North Poles. Variation changes slightly each year; if you check the compass rose on any nautical chart, it will tell you how much.

With the aid of the magnetic compass, men have been navigating the high seas since the age of exploration. It works. But my story points up a problem that particularly afflicts cruising motorboats today. Because an owner is forced to mount his magnetic compass and his electronics in the very same wheelhouse, and because that wheelhouse is often small, the magnetic compass often turns out to be just as useless as the one on the *Conception*. The reason for this is that an electronics installation can produce magnetic compass error that is every bit as serious as any produced by a cargo of drill pipe.

A motorboat owner may also want to interface or connect his compass to his electronics so the loran, for example, can have a constant heading with which to do navigational computations. A magnetic compass is not suited to this sort of use. Magnetic compasses are fine for modern speedboats, runabouts, and coastal cruisers that carry little in the way of electronics and have no need to interface with same. But for big motorboats, or even small ones making long passages, something else is needed.

Except in a few cases, like the *Conception*'s, commercial boats all have gyrocompasses to complement their magnetic compasses. Unfortunately, gyros are too expensive and complicated to be practical for anything but the largest of yachts. A fairly recent introduction to the marine scene, the flux-gate compass, is suitable for the majority of big cruising motorboats.

To understand what a flux-gate compass is, you've first got to know a little bit about the way a magnetic compass works. Although there are considerable differences in size, complexity, and accuracy, all magnetic compasses are but variations on a theme, which begins with a waterproof housing, a clear material over the top of the instrument that enables the navigator to see what's going on inside.

The housing contains a circular card, with 360 degrees printed on it, balanced very precisely on a needle. The housing is filled with a clear, viscous liquid that damps the motion of the card while it buoys it up; this reduces the friction of the needle against the card.

(Because it won't freeze and is easily obtained, isopropyl alcohol was once the liquid used. But tippling helmsmen were a problem. Before a switch was made to today's glycerin, many were the magnetic compasses that froze and broke, at least in the colder, lower latitudes, because some merry helmsman had drained his compass to the dregs and replaced the alcohol with water.)

How does a magnetic compass work? Motion is imparted to the compass card by bar magnets attached beneath it. These magnets are constantly trying to align themselves with the lines of magnetic flux that encircle the earth and pass through the magnetic North Pole. All of this hoopla, of course, is subject to deviation and variation.

The flux-gate compass is entirely different from the magnetic compass. Because it is electronic, it is not subject to deviation error. Moreover, it's more accurate. Compared to a flux-gate, a magnetic compass is slow to respond and, once it does respond, it may take a while to settle down on a new heading.

With highly specialized electronic components, flux-gate compasses actually determine the bearing of the lines of magnetic flux encircling the world. Because of their complex electronic nature, they are more expensive than magnetic compasses, but they are worth the price. They give the navigator magnetic heading information rapidly, precisely, and, most important, with a steady consistency that can be applied to an interface, say, with an autopilot. Had the *Point Conception* been equipped with a flux-gate compass, I could have navigated much more efficiently and with considerably less strain on my nervous system. I am sure that had they been available during his time, Magellan would have had flux-gate compasses plastered all over his ship.

The flux-gate compass makes a lot of sense for the modern cruising boat, since its sensing element and readout can be split up. The sensor can be mounted almost anywhere, so shipboard electronics, electrical wiring, and machinery never need interfere with its operation. The sensor, mounted in an out-of-the-way spot, can feed several displays at the helm and elsewhere. Of course, since the flux-gate gives a purely magnetic reading, the navigator must still correct for variation in order to get true bearings (the only bearings one uses in chart work).

Whether you outfit your vessel with a flux-gate or a magnetic compass, and I would recommend both (at least on larger boats), you will need to mount

There's no excuse not to have a compass aboard a boat. If you don't have a gyro-compass, a flux-gate, or even a magnetic compass at the helm, use a hand-bearing model. A hand-bearing model will work just fine as long as you keep it away from sources of compass error, like pocketknives and lorans.

the device with certain precautions in mind. Place the compass where the helmsman can see it when he is sitting comfortably. Also, mount the compass where it will be out of the weather as much as possible. And if your compass is magnetic, put it where it will be least subject to deviation error, meaning well away from metal, electronic devices, and electrical wiring.

Never make the mistake of assuming that you can mount a magnetic compass anywhere and then simply rely on it. Once it's installed, check its accuracy. See if it agrees with the bearings of some of the ranges on your chart. If it doesn't, you're going to have to "compensate" your compass, a process that involves physically turning small screws around in the compass base to make the instrument accurate. Directions usually come with the compass when you purchase it.

One final point. Harking back to the story in chapter 3 about the poor devils tooling around the Gulf of Mexico looking for diesel fuel, never lay your pocket-knife or any other metal object next to a compass and expect to get an accurate reading, much less get home before dark.

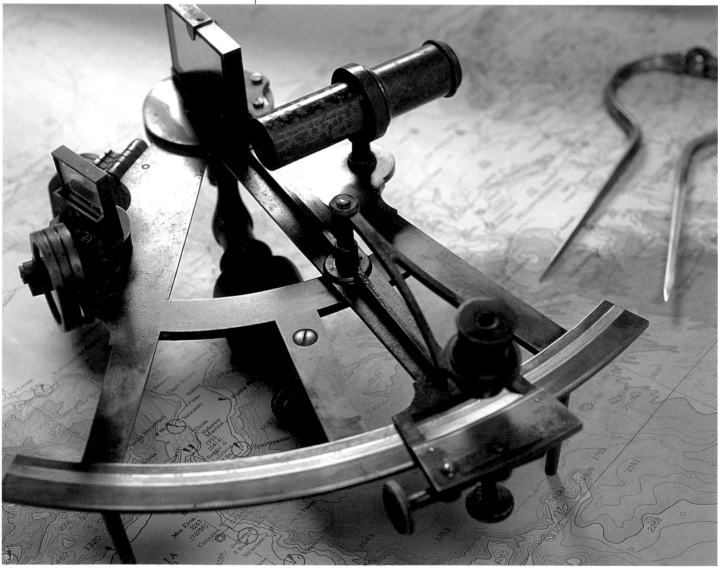

© Allan Weitz

ELECTRONIC NAVIGATIONAL DEVICES: LORAN, SATNAV, AND GPS

No discussion of important electronic equipment would be complete without some mention of electronic aids to navigation. There are three crucial devices that, in conjunction with a chart, tell you where you are, easily, succinctly, and reliably. Most of my boating has involved navigational aids that were simple, and simple aids are the devices I recommend.

Let's start with the loran, which refers to a system of navigation in which pulsed signals sent out by shore-based stations are used to help the navigator determine his position. Because loran C relies on signals from land, it is adequate for coastal navigation only. Its reliability is questionable beyond fifty miles (80 km) offshore, although I've used it at distances of more than one hundred miles (160 km) from land. The price of lorans has come down considerably since their introduction in the early 1970s.

Today's lorans will interface with autopilots and electronic chart plotters, and, theoretically, can navigate just about automatically, using preprogrammed waypoints, or points designated in latitude and longitude toward which one can steer. I have seen a loran/autopilot interface on a motoryacht navigate through a preestablished course with amazing precision. This is all well and good, of course, but you must remember that a loran has less judgment than a good dog. An autopilot interface with a loran is handy, but no reasonable person will allow it to make course changes alone.

As I said, I'm in favor of simple electronics without all the glitzy features, like a memory capable of storing a million way points. The only luxury I feel is absolutely necessary on a loran is the conversion of loran time differences (TDs) to latitude and longitude.

We don't have the time to discuss the theory of loran here and exactly what TDs are. It will be sufficient to say that you have to use TDs in conjunction with a chart that has a system of lines or a loran grid printed over its surface. The problem with old-fashioned lorans that display only TDs is that charts with grids are not always available for every nook and cranny of the world covered by loran; charts with latitude and longitude are common just about everywhere.

The coastal cruising crowd knows that while a compass and radio are probably the two most important pieces of equipment a boat should be outfitted with, loran ranks a close third. Before you buy loran, try using it at the store. Many electronics dealers will have a unit set up to simulate actual operation. Like any other piece of electronic equipment, a loran should be easy to use. I've had the pleasure of working with some that you could figure out in a matter of minutes, with or without the manual. I've also used complicated models, sold with equally complex and thoroughly confusing manuals that were so inaccessible to the average reader that one wonders if they weren't fraught with more symbolism and intricate construction than *Anna Karenina*. Certainly the modern motorboatman has little enough time to enjoy his sport. He doesn't want to devote a solid week to reading about how to get his loran to work.

courtesy Si-Tex

When initially introduced to recreational boating, loran C required the use of special charts with overlays or grids. Today's sets read out in latitude and longitude, and are compatible with standard-issue charts.

For those who cruise long distances from land, where a loran will simply not suffice, there is a non-electronic means of determining one's position. It is the oldest means of finding out where you are, out of sight of land—the sextant. In a nutshell, it measures very accurately the angle from the horizon to a celestial body, whether it be the sun, the moon, a star, or one of the planets. This angle, coupled with an accurate measurement of time, can produce a line of position. Two or three lines of position produce a fix or presumed location on a chart. I've worked aboard vessels where, on international voyages, a sextant was used to cross-check electronic positioning, though such vessels were in the minority.

Books have been written about sextants and what to do with them. Learning how to use a sextant—or more precisely, how to make the calculations necessary to consummate one's relationship with the sextant by getting a fix—can be an arduous process.

However, for serious offshore motorboatmen, knowing how to use a sextant is very helpful. Should you be several hundred miles from anywhere and your electronics package fails you, you'll be glad you brought a sextant on the trip, along with your sight-reduction tables and a copy of *The Nautical Almanac*.

If you want to learn how to use a sextant, the best way is probably to take a course. Schools that offer preparatory courses for commercial licensing exams offer courses in celestial navigation. I learned to use a sextant from an instructor initially, and then practiced at sea until after a couple of months I became comfortable with this method of navigation that is basically a very precise mixture of paperwork and physical activity.

courtesy Furuno

Positioning devices using GPS satellites are the wave of the future. Unlike satnav, a system that uses the lower-level Transit Satellite System and is subject to breaks in coverage, GPS sets offer amazing accuracy anywhere, twenty-four hours a day.

Learning how to use a satnav (satellite navigator) or a GPS (Global Positioning System) is much easier than learning how to use a sextant. Satnav and GPS are navigational computers that compute latitude and longitude based on signals received from satellites. While all three instruments produce essentially the same information for the navigator, satnav and GPS navigational computers are faster and more accurate in most cases.

Satnav was first introduced in the late 1960s. It relies on a constellation of five satellites officially known as the Transit Satellite System, which orbit about six hundred miles (960 km) above the surface of the earth. Satnav would be the perfect replacement for coastal-exclusive loran, except for two points. The first and most important point is that satnav is not capable of continuous positioning; it calculates fixes by measuring Doppler shift of a satellite as it passes overhead. Doppler shift is the perceived change in a frequency of a signal, whether that signal be the horn of a passing diesel locomotive or the energy emitted by a transit satellite.

Because there are only five satellites aloft in the transit system, it's not unusual for a few hours, even several hours, to elapse between fixes. The infrequency of satellite passes is generally not a major problem far out at sea where satnavs work fine. If the nearest reef is a thousand miles (1,600 km) away, the navigator doesn't much care when he gets his satnav fixes, as long as several are received each day. But when you're navigating coastwise, trying to find a specific channel or sea buoy, or avoid a reef, the satnav falls short. I've gone as much as six hours without getting a good fix out of a satnav.

To be really accurate, a satnav requires accurate speed and course input data from your vessel. This is because its measurements are made sequentially, not instantly. The more rapid the motion of the vessel, the more important that it be entered into the satnav's calculations. Some units are set up to receive data from a boat's compass and "log," a speed-measuring device. Some manufacturers provide their own compasses and logs with the units they sell, and some satnavs work pretty well with only an estimated speed and course programmed in.

What we have established thus far is this. Loran is excellent for navigation of coasts, and satnav is fine for navigating the open sea. Both devices have drawbacks. Now we're going to talk about a navigation device that has none of the drawbacks of loran and satnav and all the advantages. It's called a Global Positioning System (GPS).

Today, depth-sounders are almost as complex as international politics. Some manufacturers claim their models not only can tell you how many fish are under your boat, but exactly what species they are.

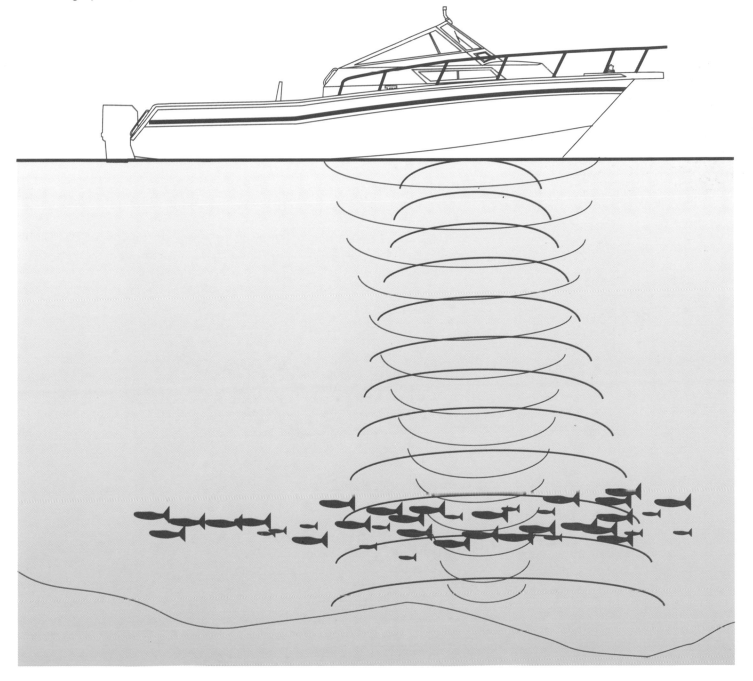

Someday, GPS will probably replace satnav and maybe even loran. Like satnav, GPS is a satellite-type system. However, GPS is more sophisticated than satnav, with twice as many satellites aloft in much higher orbits, and promises incredible accuracy at sea or coastwise, uninterrupted, twenty-four hours a day. As yet, the fine tuning of the GPS system is not complete. Not all the satellites are up, but the prices of the equipment certainly are. Using loran for coastal trips and satnav for extended voyages will continue to make economical sense until the GPS system is complete and prices for the equipment have come down to earth.

DEPTH-SOUNDERS: SOUNDING THE DEPTHS OF THE DEEP

A depth-sounder is another important and quite essential piece of equipment aboard any boat. A depth-sounder is one of the best means of keeping you from running aground and can help you navigate. On some runabouts and other small boats with very little draft, you can probably get by without one, contingent, of course, upon your "local knowledge," or the knowledge you have of the water you'll be using the boat in. But on larger boats, which will travel unfamiliar waters, a depth-sounder is a necessity.

The trend in electronics today seems to be toward integration. In other words, a positioning device interfaced with an electronic plotter (below) is sold as a single unit.

NavGraphic II GPS·LORAN

Depth-sounders are aptly named. They send a high-frequency sound signal from a transducer (or fitting on the bottom of your boat) down to the bottom of the water. The signal then bounces back, is received by the transducer, and routed to the depth-sounder itself, where the distance to the bottom is computed and displayed, using the simple formula: D (distance) = R (rate) × T (time).

Ten or fifteen years ago, almost all depth-sounders displayed their readings on a scrolling paper roll that was viewed on the face of the unit. Today, depth can be displayed on paper, on electronic screens, or digitally. I prefer the digital units because they're cheaper than the other models. I also prefer models that don't offer a whole lot of extraneous features, such as readouts for water temperature, speed, and so on; this preference is in keeping with my belief that one should never consolidate electronic and navigational equipment. To me consolidation means that, should one unit fail, the others may also.

If you intend to mount your own transducer on the bottom of your boat, remember the following: Never mount it near areas of the bottom that are subject to turbulence, such as around the transom, or just abaft some sort of through-hull fitting, like a raw-water engine intake. Mount the transducer on the outside of the hull bottom, not on the inside; the thickness of fiberglass between the transducer surface and the water is enough to distort the signal.

Additionally, unless your boat has an absolutely flat bottom, mount the transducer as close to the centerline of the vessel as possible, so it will be "looking" straight down and ahead. This prevents a bias to right or left, caused by the dead rise of the bottom, and will prevent the depth-sounder from giving you bogus readings.

The depth-sounder also can help you navigate. If you're lost—it happens to the best of us sometimes—you can use the depth of water you're in as a clue to your location. For example, if you're in two fathoms of water (twelve feet, or 3.6 m), look for two-fathom soundings on the chart. There will, no doubt, be many. But combine this clue with others, like a TD from your loran or a bearing off a lighthouse, and presto! You suddenly have a fairly decent idea of where you're at.

Which brings to mind an important point. Over time, most motorboatmen learn never to base their navigation on one source of information, even though that source may be historically reliable. Your loran may work fine. But don't rely on it implicitly. Occasionally check the positioning information it gives you against what your depth-sounder reads, particularly when traveling in shallow water. Do the soundings or depth notations on your chart for your probable position match the figures on the depth-sounder? If not, there's something amiss. It's time to stop and get your bearings.

Like most everything else associated with motorboats today, depth-sounders have gotten rather complex over the past couple of years. Video-recording depth-sounders are popular among fishermen. Manufacturers claim that some models can not only spot fish below a boat but make a positive identification, right down to the size and species. Why anybody would want to so thoroughly remove the mystery, the element of surprise, from the sport of fishing is beyond me. Everybody wants to be a spy these days.

Courtesy of Si-Tex

The age of paper is drawing to a close, or at least it sometimes seems so. Most modern depth-sounder/fish finders have electronic screens that provide the user with readings for depth of water, temperature, bottom shape, and location of schools of fish. Just fifteen years ago, most depth-sounders used paper rolls and mechanically operated recording pens to convey such information.

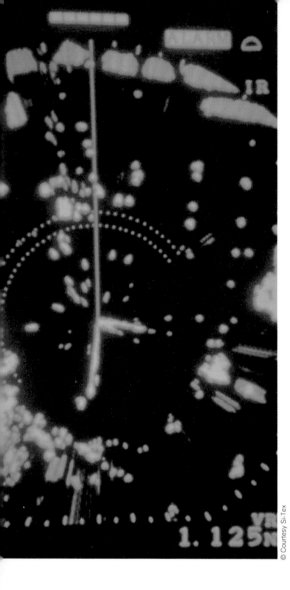

© Courtesy Si-Tex

A couple of important facts about radar: 1) Radar waves are unhealthy. Never stand in front of turning scanners (top). 2) Learning how to interpret the "picture" on a radar screen takes long hours of practice.

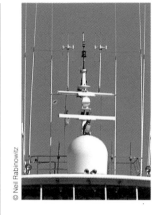

© Neil Rabinowitz

RADAR...THE SEEING-EYE DOG

So far we've discussed various pieces of electronic gear that just about any boat should have, whether its venue be inland waterways or the sea. Now I'm going to talk briefly about radar, a very convenient electronic aid to navigation that, for my money, is not an absolute necessity, although radar on a foggy night is certainly worth its weight in gold.

Unfortunately, the amount of gold involved may not measure up to the purchase price (the cheapest radar sells for about $1,500). For some motorboatmen, it's cheaper to skip buying a radar set and, when fog or any other sort of decreased-visibility situation sets in, set in with it. Plain old waiting is a time-honored and honorable method of dealing with visibility problems, espoused even by some motorboatmen who *do* have radar.

Every commercial boat I ever worked on had radar, usually two, sometimes three devices. Aboard my own recreational boats, I've never had a radar installed, primarily because I couldn't afford one. Still, I've enjoyed a lot of solid motorboating fun without mishap.

A radar works something like a depth-sounder. A high-frequency radio wave is emitted from a rotating "scanner," or barlike horizontal structure located above the superstructure of the vessel. The wave is reflected from something solid on the water, like a point of land or an eight-hundred-foot (240-m) tanker, and captured again by the scanner, then subsequently processed by the radar set itself. The radar observer sees the object as a blip or "target" on the cathode ray tube (CRT) of the radar in the wheelhouse. (There are plenty of manuals that can explain how to tune a radar and how to use it.)

I know an old charter-boat captain who calls his radar "the seeing-eye dog," which is essentially what all radars are. Radar waves are not deterred by darkness and they're not deterred by fog, haze, rain, or snow, although the radar's ability to work well in the latter depends to a considerable extent upon density. I've seen heavy rain, snow, and even fog "white out" a radar as well as a blindfold.

The problem with the radar is that once a navigator spends several thousand dollars on one, he begins to think he is invincible. This is *not* the case.

Radar is a very handy tool, but it cannot be relied upon to work all the time. It will not prevent your boat from striking something in the fog, particularly if that something is a wooden boat, wood being a material that produces a very faint radar return, if any.

Some years ago, I heard a story about a man who called himself "a professional mariner." At one point in the story, he was reported to have felt betrayed. "But I couldn't see it on my radar," he said. He was responsible for hitting a wooden shrimp boat on a clear, moonlit night when visibility was excellent.

AUTOPILOTS: THE EASY WAY TO STEER

Autopilots are the purview of hard-core cruising people and sportfishermen who make long treks to their fishing grounds. Autopilots are mostly found on large inboard boats with hydraulic or some other form of mechanical steering gear. Recently, autopilots for small, stern-driven boats have been introduced. Whether enough small-boat owners, given the type of boating they do, will feel that the relatively high cost of these units is warranted remains to be seen.

On a cruising boat, an autopilot is not absolutely necessary, but it is extremely handy. For one thing, an autopilot frees the helmsman up so he can easily navigate, use the VHF, and scan the horizon at his leisure. If properly adjusted, an autopilot also will steer a better course than any human helmsman. A good autopilot makes for less running time between waypoints and better fuel economy.

In most cases, autopilots use either gyrocompasses or flux-gate compasses to sense the vessel's direction and maintain it. Autopilots also can be interfaced with lorans, satnavs, or almost any other positioning system so that they will steer through a sequence of waypoints.

You can buy hand-held control units on long cords, so you can change your autopilot's course while doing something else. I don't see any reason why anyone would want a remote control on his autopilot. Although there are claims that, armed with a remote, a helmsman can climb his boat's mast and steer while negotiating reefs that can better be seen from some height, it all sounds like advertising hype to me. I've never done it. And I don't know a soul who has.

Be cautious with your autopilot, just as you would with a radar set. Just when you're bragging about your autopilot's stellar qualities, such as consistency, sensitivity, and endurance, it's going to err, maybe even refuse to work. And if you interface your autopilot with a positioning device, such as a loran or satnav, and then proceed to allow this dynamic duo to steer you around the ocean, keep a close eye on things. Remember, like any computer, an autopilot is no better than the information it is given.

Don't put yourself in the position of a third-mate friend of mine who let his autopilot nearly scare him out of his wits one night. Strictly against everything that's holy, the mate was playing chess while on watch, with the helmsman in the chartroom behind the wheelhouse. The ship was on autopilot.

Between games, just to assure himself that the ship was safely pointed in the right direction, the mate decided to step out into the wheelhouse to take a look around.

Imagine his shock. The eight-hundred-footer (240 m) under his charge was in the process of turning around, making a big circle. An electrical glitch in the engine room had knocked the pilot out, and the ship was swinging about with its rudders frozen.

Your autopilot should be part of a practical, easy-to-use electronics layout, like the one pictured here.

© Allan Weitz

Some people mistakenly believe that the weight alone of an anchor secures it to a specific piece of sea, lake, or river bottom. It is, however, the arrowhead-shaped flukes of most anchors that, in conjunction with their weight, give them real holding power.

The story concludes with a few salty phrases describing how quickly the wheelsman and mate resumed their separate stations in the wheelhouse and how gently the ship was returned to her proper course, so as not to disturb the captain, who, as luck would have it, was sleeping soundly in his cabin below.

ANCHORS AWEIGH

The last item in our chapter on basic gear is an anchor, or better yet, anchors. Don't forget that for each one, you'll need plenty of rode (anchor rope). An anchor without a proper rode is about as pointless as an existentialist novel.

Being at anchor, especially at sunset or sunrise, is one of the great pleasures of the motorboating way of life. Eating lunch on the hook has a leisurely quality to it, completely unmatched by the hurriedness of eating lunch on the run, for example, or the uncertain feeling of dining while adrift. Too often, anchoring is regarded as work only, its pleasures forgotten.

One of the most popular anchors is the Danforth type, which has sharp and pivoting flukes that dig into the bottom when pull is exerted on the stock. Even though Danforth-type anchors are usually made of galvanized steel, they are light and easy to handle because of the way they are constructed. Sometimes, they are made of stainless steel, which, of course, makes them stronger but more expensive.

Plow anchors are also popular. Usually made of galvanized steel as well, they hold the bottom under just about any conditions. Their flukes come together in a plowlike point, and the shank is usually pivoted. Because of this pivot, plows usually stay buried, even with changes in the direction of pull resulting from changes in wind direction or tide.

Another type of anchor is the Bruce, which was initially designed for use on oil rigs in the North Sea. It is a burying type, like the plow.

The last type of anchor is the kedge, which we won't spend much time on since it's not used on many recreational vessels today. This anchor simply hooks the bottom and looks something like a three-dimensional version of the gold anchors that sailors often wear around their necks. Kedge anchors are cumbersome because of their unwieldy shape and hard to stow.

The number of anchors you carry on your boat depends to a large extent on its size. Because they spend their time either gadding about or tied to a dock, some small runabouts and speedboats can get by with no anchor at all. Almost all other boats have at least one. If your boat's thirty feet (9 m) or more in length, it's recommended that you have three anchors: a primary, a smaller secondary, and a still smaller "lunch hook."

The best primary anchor is the plow, because, as I mentioned, it holds in all sorts of bottom conditions and resists breaking loose with shifts of wind and current. The best secondary anchor is probably the Danforth type, simply because it's light and stows easily. The lunch hook should probably be the Danforth type as well, but smaller, and is recommended for the same reasons.

courtesy Fortress Marine Anchors

The best method of setting anchors occurs on bigger boats outfitted with bow pulpits. The bow pulpit is a small platform that extends beyond the bow, on the centerline of the boat, and is enclosed by stainless-steel safety rails. Probably the nicest anchoring systems entail pulpits that are set up with two or more separate anchor chocks, or fairleads, small metal fittings that hold and direct anchor rode to the cleats, where it is fastened. Thus, two anchors can be stowed at, and worked from, the bow. This way, both anchors can be deployed quickly if necessary. You needn't go around the whole boat searching for the secondary anchor, which may have worked its way into a wonderful hiding place.

Placing the secondary and its rode in a cardboard box or plastic milk crate may be fine, but it doesn't work well if you need to set two hooks in a blow or if you're trying to anchor over difficult holding ground.

Except for high-performance and very small watercraft, just about every boat you can buy is going to have some sort of "rope locker" on the bow to stow anchor rode in. I strongly suggest that you buy a boat with a pad eye (or some other kind of fastener with a hole) inside this locker so that the bitter, or unsecured, end of your anchor rode can be secured there. If your boat does not have such a pad eye, install some kind of substitute. Otherwise, you may drop the hook someday, then discover that you've lost the whole kit and caboodle, anchor and rode. I've witnessed such a loss, and it is usually accompanied by a look of bemusement that rapidly turns to horror, with dollar signs ringing up in the eyes like a mad slot machine.

A bow pulpit with anchor roller, striker plate, and life rails makes anchor handling a lot easier than it might be otherwise.

While nylon line makes excellent anchor rode, it is also very handy for towing, as any rescue boat skipper will tell you.

© Neil Rabinowitz

Notice the electric windlass at the base of this bow pulpit; it makes picking up the anchor easy. All you have to do is push a button.

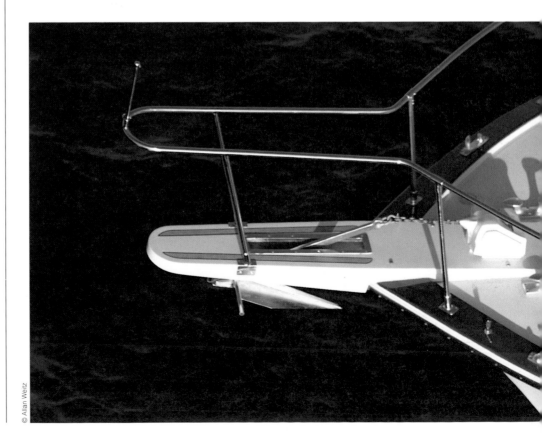

© Allan Weitz

When equipping your boat with an anchor, give some thought to installing an anchor windlass—a small, electrically powered machine that will pull rope or chain up like a locomotive. You especially need a windlass if you have a bad back, or if you plan to cruise with an inexperienced crew.

My wife could well have been numbered among the inexperienced the first time we attempted to pull the hook due to worsening sea conditions. There are two jobs to pulling the hook on a thirty-two-foot (9.6-m) cruiser, both of which must be done simultaneously. Since my wife refused to operate the controls of the boat from the bridge (one job), the only alternative was for her to pull the hook herself (the other job).

To cut a long and grim tale short, communication broke down. Tempers grew short. Actually, the communication problem was not all my fault, given my hearing difficulties that are due to an injury sustained while I was fighting for my country, risking life and limb in the twisted, far-off jungles of Southeast Asia. Ahem.

There's little use going into the whole fracas in detail. The upshot of the whole thing was this: My wife now refuses to travel aboard any motorboat, sailboat, ship, raft, barge, or ferry that is not equipped with a windlass that lifts the anchor, or anchors, automatically.

There's one more item to discuss regarding anchors: rode. The best line for anchor rode is nylon. For powerboats, the best or at least most frequently used nylon is the hard-laid three-strand variety. Rode, as well as dock lines, should be at least five-eighths of an inch (1.6 cm) thick. Nylon rode makes the most sense for powerboats since all-chain rode, when stored in a rope locker on the bow of most any boat, is going to adversely affect performance. One of the last items you want aboard a boat built to plane is a lot of extra weight at the bow.

Although your anchor rode may be nylon, make sure a fair length of chain, about twenty to thirty feet (6 to 9 m) of it, is used to connect it to the ring at the top of the anchor stock. Use a shackle to do this. Then use an adjustable wrench to tighten the bolt hard, and wire it in place or use plastic twist-ties. Once the anchor is deployed, the weight of the chain causes a more horizontal tension on the anchor, better ensuring it will not break loose. Also, the chain will not chafe on the bottom and break, as line may sometimes do.

We've reached the end of our outfitting discussion, but before we move on, there are two more pieces of equipment no boat should be without: a flashlight and a basic tool kit. (There's nothing like being caught offshore with a mechanical problem and not even a proper screwdriver.) Otherwise, we've covered the motorboatman's standard equipment list. The rest of the job, outfitting your boat so that it becomes really yours, is basically a matter of taste and means. Go to it.

CHAPTER SIX

THE MOTORBOATING LIFE

courtesy Suzuki Marine

Living life to the fullest on board is not quite like living life to the fullest ashore. Certain changes are required. Motorboatmen don't dress the same, eat the same, drink the same, or even behave the same as their landlocked cousins.

In this chapter, we're going to discuss the motorboating life, hitting the high spots (and the low spots), in an attempt to describe how best to fit in, survive, and even flourish at sea.

One big difference between experienced and inexperienced motorboatmen is the way in which they react to boating advertisements, particularly the way the models are dressed in them. In my experience, I have never seen, except maybe aboard and around some Italian yachts in the Mediterranean, people dressed anything like the models in most boating advertisements.

Half of the fun of boating is the adventure of it. Getting sunburned. Or frostbitten. Although we may find it difficult to admit, real adventure often involves unpleasantness such as hard work, sweat, dirt, grease, and seasickness. So what's the best way to get dressed to go motorboating? With common sense. Nobody wears insulated foul-weather gear to stay dry during the afternoon rains in Panama in the middle of July. By the same token, nobody goes cruising the crystal waters of Georgian Bay in Lake Huron in August without a few sweatshirts and jackets on board, and maybe a pair of mittens. Basically, unless you must have the latest in fashion and color, you can buy the necessary clothing in some very non-maritime places. Motorboating calls for just a few clothing essentials, none of which can be found exclusively in maritime fashion catalogs.

In fact, few members of the motorboat majority, even when intensely involved in their sport, look much different from your average vacationing tourist. Normal attire is a pair of shorts, scuffed-up deck shoes, or perhaps an expensive pair of sneakers, and some type of durable shirt. The bottom line is that it doesn't really matter that you look fashionable while boating.

Let's face it. Living life to the fullest on board is not quite like living life to the fullest ashore.

A pair of shorts, a pair of deck shoes, a T-shirt, some sun block, sunglasses, a hat, and a rain jacket—that's all you need to have fun on a boat.

Actually, if you're going to fit in with the majority of motorboaters and you're worrying about how you look, you're missing the point. People that look too "yachty" are usually the object of gentle scorn among longtime members of the Motorboating Majority. So to fit in, don't buy anything special, except for a foul-weather jacket. Don't skimp on this item. Make sure your foul-weather jacket is of excellent quality. It should have a high collar and a simple pocket system so it doesn't take a road map to find the case for your sunglasses. For cold weather, layer sweaters or a down vest underneath.

Deck shoes: I prefer deck shoes with canvas uppers. Leather deck shoes, especially when worn without socks for any length of time, eventually begin to smell terrible. In addition, leather deck shoes are very expensive and tend to disintegrate in a habitat that includes diesel fuel. If your boat uses diesel, get a pair of rubber boots to wear for engine-room maintenance. And wear socks, or else it's likely that you're going to wind up with a pair of boots capable of throwing an aroma that will put your leather deck shoes to shame.

While we're on the subject of shoes, did you ever wonder how deck shoes came into being? And who had the idea to put all those wavy slits in the bottom? The story goes this way. In the winter of 1935, Paul Sperry noticed that his dog, Prince, was sliding less in slippery situations than people shod in ordinary shoes. He studied his pet's paws, and attempted to duplicate the tread on the bottom of a boat shoe, using a razor blade to cut a multi-dimensional pattern into a piece of crepe rubber. Today, boat shoes, inspired by Sperry's invention, are pervasive both on the waterfront and in the mall.

Some of the best deck shoes have canvas uppers and rubber bottoms. They dry much faster than leather, tend not to smell as much, and if you buy the less expensive models, are virtually disposable. You can change them every month or so. I don't know how many navy blue canvas deck shoes I've bought at factory outlets and department stores in my lifetime. But every pair's been worth it.

Outdoor clothing: Whether your clothing comes from Patagonia, EMS, Eddie Bauer, J.C. Penney, Sears, or any of several other companies, your clothing, especially your shirts, should be capable of withstanding rugged use.

Sunglasses: These are essential for protecting your eyes. Invariably, should you forget your shades on a hot day on the water, the evening will find you fighting a headache. If you're going to be doing any fishing, especially for long periods of time, you might want to buy Polaroids; they'll help you see what's going on in the water better, even if you have to look in the direction of the sun. It's also a good idea to attach your glasses to a cord that you can wear around your neck.

A pocketknife: You will be surprised at how many times a good, sharp pocketknife will come in handy. Avoid expensive knives with stainless steel blades. They take ages to sharpen but seem to dull just as quickly as high-carbon steel.

A Tilley hat: Although a Tilley hat is often associated with sailing, it is an excellent motorboating accoutrement, especially when the weather gets

rough or when the sun gets hot. There's a chin string to keep the hat on. The Canadian-made Tilley is guaranteed to last a lifetime, and feels good on your head. There are several varieties, and they are all very expensive. So don't get pushed into owning a baseball cap with a Caterpillar logo, unless you're a diesel mechanic.

Who cares about being fashionable at idyllic moments like these?

THE COMPLETE BOOK OF MOTORBOATING

There's nothing nearly as fun as rafting up, one boat tied alongside another. You can swap food, drink, and stories for days.

WINING AND DINING

It used to be that food and boats didn't mix, a state of affairs that may have something to do with the fact that alcohol and boats always have. Why this schizophrenic attitude toward food and drink? Why have motorboatmen been abhorring food on the one hand and getting completely absorbed by the realm of John Barleycorn on the other for ages?

Years ago, the attitude made a lot of sense. Food on ships was so bad a person needed a drink to take his or her mind off the taste of it. For example, a particularly unpopular ration of canned meat used to be called "Fanny Adams" by the chaps in the British navy. Why? In 1867, in England, a child, one Fanny Adams, was murdered, dismembered, and disposed of—no one knew where. The case received a lot of publicity when, a few months after the incident, a sailor discovered a button in his dinner; he or his mates called the food "Fanny Adams," and the name stuck.

The acceptance of drinking while boating lasted at least through 1964, when *Esquire* magazine's *Book of Boating* advised:

Many a mediocre cook has risen to fame through the simple but marvelously effective expedient of serving cocktails prior to sounding the dinner gong....When your yacht flies the cocktail flag while in a strange anchorage, fellow yachtsmen will raft alongside and you'll make new acquaintances....One of the easiest ways to add new flavors to simple foods afloat is to use wine. Use wine or sherry instead of the half cup of liquid called for in cakes, cookies, pudding or pie mixes, gelatins and salads (choose red or white wines depending on the color of the gelatin), in spaghetti sauce, canned baked beans, and soups.

Needless to say, advice like this gives motorboating a bad name, especially these days, when driving while intoxicated, whether on the water or off, is such a problem. If motorboatmen were to take the *Esquire* book at its word, it seems that they'd have to abstain from both drinking *and* eating in order to operate their boats safely and legally.

It's a mystery why driving while intoxicated on our nation's highways was for many years considered a serious matter and the same sort of irresponsible behavior was indulgently viewed as an inevitable adjunct to the seagoing life. Driving a motorboat drunk is at least as dangerous as driving an automobile drunk. This is more true now than it ever was, in light of the fact that many boats today are capable of speeds in excess of sixty miles (96 km) per hour.

But don't get the idea that I'm trying to start up a maritime version of the old temperance movement. Nothing could be further from the truth. Alcohol indeed does have a place aboard the modern motorboat. Most cruisers in the midsize range, in fact, are equipped with wet bars and ice makers to accommodate the often ritualistic use of alcohol on the high seas.

I don't suppose there's anything so comradely as sitting around a table on a motorboat in the evening, telling sea stories while wetting one's hawse. Or sitting in an anchorage, watching the sun go down, glass in hand. Rum used to be the drink of the sea, although today it seems as if any old thing will do.

© Allan Weitz

Feeding the crew is a big job, a task often accomplished in a little galley. Experience and a few of the tips mentioned in this chapter should allow you to get a lot of mileage out of limited space and a minimal amount of equipment.

Just remember: If you go ashore to splice the main brace, be careful coming back. Most drownings aboard commercial vessels occur at the dock, or rather, between the dock and the ship. Drunken sailors find gangways slippery. Then they find their separate ways to Davy Jones's locker.

Today, due to refrigeration, eating a meal aboard a modern motorboat does not require that either the dinner or the diner be liberally dosed with alcohol beforehand. Here are a few recommendations to make your motorboat cookery turn out well:

1) Buy Teflon-covered pots and pans. They will not last as long as stainless steel, but they will be much easier to use. For the saltwater enthusiast, everything else in the galley—knives, eating utensils, even the can opener—should be stainless steel. High-carbon steel rusts.

2) Use heavy, simple china plates and cups that can be replaced easily. Don't form the mistaken notion that the plastic stuff, so-called yachting ware, is perfect for boats just because it's got a non-skid rubber ring on the bottom and a picture of a mermaid or anchor on its surface. You can equip china with a non-skid bottom: Buy a tube of silicone, run a bead of the compound around the bottom of a cup or plate, and let it dry. Also, plastic plates get very scratched from just a little use, and even with their non-skid feature, they weigh so little that they don't stay on the table very well at all in a heavy sea. China is heavier and lasts longer.

3) If you're looking to buy a cruising motorboat, remember that a large sink in the galley, rather than a small one, is preferable. A good, usable sink will be about a foot (30 cm) deep. In a galley equipped with a small shallow sink, you're going to get dishwater all over yourself and the cabin sole, or floor, even when doing the dishes in a fairly quiet anchorage.

4) Avoid kerosene stoves. I owned one of these stainless steel wonders for several years, and would recommend their use only to people who don't like to eat, don't need to eat, and do most of their boating in close proximity to a hook-and-ladder company.

The theory of most kerosene stoves is the same. You fill a preheating ring beneath the burner head with alcohol and light it. If you don't use enough alcohol, the kerosene doesn't vaporize properly and you can forget about supper until the ring cools down enough for a refill. Never, in any case, try to refill a hot ring.

If you use too much alcohol, it spills over the bottom of the stove and, when ignited, may fill your galley with leaping flames, sometimes igniting curtains and facial hair. Alcohol, which is colorless and hard to see, may even drip down the side of the cabinetry onto the cabin sole. Unless you've got the self-discipline of a fakir, burning alcohol on canvas deck shoes can ruin a meal.

My stove never really produced a meal without turning the overhead black with soot and stinking up the boat, no matter how clean the burners were. My stove had an oven that never produced anything.

5) Alcohol stoves, while producing considerably less heat than kerosene, are much safer than kerosene and 100 percent more reliable. I've owned several Origo models, and they all worked well. An even better choice is the alcohol/electric stove. Add a microwave oven, which can run off of your boat's generator or shore power, and you're really cooking.

6) Which brings up the subject of propane. Propane has a lot of advantages. It is hot, fast, and uncomplicated. Its disadvantages are that it is highly explosive and heavier than air, so that it can flow like a liquid, seeking the lowest level, which turns out to be the bilge areas in most cases, beneath the engine or engines. Hitting the ignition key with a bilge full of propane has a predictable effect.

If you must install a propane stove aboard your boat, make sure the tank is stored in a locker outside the boat's cabin, that the locker is completely isolated from the cabin, that it has an overboard drain, and that it has a very tight lid. Additionally, make sure that regulators, pressure gauges, shutoff valves, and remote solenoids are installed properly and are well maintained. And, although it may seem silly to suggest such foolishness, never check for leaks with an open flame.

Pretty, isn't it? Although everything looks splendid, this certainly isn't your typical at-sea dining situation. Under some circumstances, eating beans from a can may be just as romantic.

THE MOTORBOATING LIFE

SEASICKNESS AND WHAT TO DO ABOUT IT

Seasickness, or *mal de mer,* is a democratic illness. If you've got it, by George, you've simply got it, no matter what your station in life. And don't ever think that seasickness results from severe sea conditions only. It can accompany the least little movement of the mighty ocean, as long as that movement is prolonged. My father once got seasick during a tour of a replica of the *Mayflower,* which was docked at Plymouth, Massachusetts.

The most concentrated case of seasickness I ever encountered occurred during a hurricane in the Gulf of Mexico. I was working on a boat that was tied up in Lake Charles, Louisiana, waiting out the storm. We were all playing poker in the galley when the dispatcher called on the company radio, telling us we had to evacuate an oil rig immediately. Winds were already too high to get the men stationed there off via helicopter.

We scrambled out to the rig, running darn near full tilt under outrageous conditions. Once we'd arrived, getting the men aboard proved difficult, but we succeeded.

Imagine what it must have been like for these guys. Within a few wild and fearful minutes, they were transferred from a stable platform with its legs firmly planted on the bottom of the Gulf of Mexico, to a rocking, rolling supply boat in the throes of fifteen- to twenty-foot (4.5- to 6-m) seas.

Even guys that said they usually didn't get sick, got sick. It was a regular free-for-all of seasickness. On the way back to land, I wandered from the wheelhouse down to the galley for a few moments. It looked like a battleground, strewn with bodies. Eventually, we had to open the doors of the wheelhouse to allow the rising fumes to escape.

What is seasickness? It's a difficulty in the inner ear that causes the rest of your body to think you've been poisoned. When poisoning occurs, of course, your body reacts by trying to get rid of the "poison" as quickly as possible. This process is accompanied by physical sensations that can be fairly compared, peristaltically speaking, with a tidal wave. Caused by even the most gentle motions of a boat, seasickness can worsen with increased motion. Other things make it worse, too, such as drinking coffee or inhaling the horrible odors of fried food and diesel fuel.

Remedies? Eating crackers. Watching the horizon. Taking medications in pill or intravenous form, *before going aboard,* or, in less extremely affected persons, before the approach of a bad storm. Once the malady has taken over, there's little chance of keeping a pill down long enough to let it do any good.

A recent introduction to the field of cures is the Sea-Band, a set of small elastic bands with plastic buttons inside them that put pressure on the *Nei-Kuan* acupuncture point inside both wrists. This involves no drugs, so there's no drowsiness.

Intestinal fortitude has little bearing on whether a person will succumb to seasickness. This age-old malady can cause heartburn and stomach distress in even the most robust individual.

And then there's scopolamine, which is absorbed through bandage-like patches that are usually stuck behind the ear. A doctor's prescription is required. I've never used the drug but have been told that sometimes the feelings it induces are almost as bad as the feelings one gets from seasickness.

The best remedy of all—and I think anyone who has suffered from seasickness will agree—is to just get off the darn boat, preferably by stepping onto dry land.

Seasickness does not result from severe sea conditions only; in fact, it can accompany the least little movement of the almighty ocean.

IF MISS MANNERS WERE HERE...

We'll get into the Rules of the Road in the next chapter. In the meantime, here are some lesser-known rules of etiquette, but fairly important ones nevertheless.

1) It used to be that motorboatmen were cautioned not to stare at other boats. This is a suggestion often ignored today and, I think, rightly so. What's the harm in ogling another person's runabout, or even some of the folks on it? Society's opened up today. Stare all you like. Smile. Wave. You only live once.

2) Never pass by a vessel in distress without offering to lend a hand.

3) Don't throw garbage, or any other junk in the water. I deign to emphasize that plastic garbage, particularly the harnesses that hold beer and soda cans together, should be disposed of ashore. I've seen too many sea animals half-strangled by these things.

4) When encountering NO WAKE ZONES, slow down.

5) Don't stare at a person trying to dock a boat, especially if he is new at the game; you're liable to unnerve the poor soul.

6) Given the proliferation of strange people in the world, carry a gun on long blue-water trips. Aboard the oceangoing tugs I used to work, vessels that traveled all over the world, Winchester repeating rifles were hung in every wheelhouse.

Several years ago, I read a story in a Venezuelan newspaper about some heavily armed pirates who boarded a boat just off the Venezuelan coast. According to a witness who escaped, the pirates sent the unarmed owner of the hapless vessel swimming with an outboard motor tied around his neck. The witness, who apparently slipped over the side and made it to shore unnoticed, reported that the pirates enjoyed murdering people this way.

If you plan to travel the high seas, carry weapons, with the proviso, of course, that you know how to use them safely. Generally speaking, most foreign countries require that you declare any weapons when clearing customs. Failure to do so can result in your arrest and the confiscation of your boat.

The chances that you will ever have to use a firearm to defend yourself and your crew at sea are slim. I certainly don't intend to imply that the Caribbean Sea, or any other body of water, is crawling with bloodthirsty crazies. But why wind up sorry when you might just as easily have been safe?

CHAPTER SEVEN

SAFETY ON THE WATER

GUARD

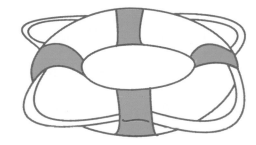

When I was training to be a Great Lakes pilot, an instructor once told me that accidents don't usually happen to neophytes. Pilots who are new to the job, who are nervously aware of the potential for error in every little aspect of it, rarely get into trouble. The reason for this is simple: New pilots have a very low level of comfort aboard ship. Although they may be quite competent, they constantly worry about making mistakes.

Accidents, my instructor said, are much more likely to happen to seafarers who consider themselves capable, well trained, and on top of any situation. Those that are comfortable with their work to the point of complacency are more likely to get into trouble.

Not only is this true of piloting vessels on the Great Lakes, it's true of just about every type of recreational boating as well. The majority of accidents occur not because people don't know what to do, but because they simply don't bother to do it. In this chapter, we're going to look at things that you, as a motorboatman, should know about, care about, or learn about, so that you can safely enjoy the sport.

GOING BACK TO SCHOOL

The most basic thing a freshly launched motorboatman, and perhaps even a more experienced one, can do to ensure safety aboard his boat is to get some formal motorboating education. One of the best ways to do this is to take some sort of boating course, government sponsored or otherwise, which will be chockablock with material on boating safety. Once he's completed the course, the motorboatman should attempt to follow its dictates afterward to the best of his ability. The Power Squadron teaches a boating course to over thirty-four thousand boatmen and their families each year, in close to five hundred different locations throughout the United States and overseas.

Speed on the water is great fun. Too much of a good thing can be too much, however, and can engender a citation.

A recent introduction to the squadron's repertoire is a video version of the boating course. If you're just getting into motorboating, or even if you've been motorboating for a while and you absolutely can't get to a spot where the course is offered, buy the video and watch it a few times.

If you are an "old hand" at boats, with a lot of water under your keel, you might not benefit from entry-level courses. There are commercial schools in many countries that prepare candidates to take various commercial licensing examinations. Such schools offer everything from charterboat-captain licensing courses to courses that prepare you to sit for a master's license.

If you're interested in broadening your horizons and sharpening your motorboating skills, you might contact one of these licensing schools and make some arrangements to take one of the many courses available, either through the mail or via an actual classroom situation. Then maybe you'd like to get your sea time properly documented and sit for your own license.

FIRE... FIRE... FIRE

What should you do in case of fire? Your safety and the safety of your passengers may someday hinge on how well you know the answer to this question. On board any motorboat, the most dangerous place to have a fire is in the machinery spaces or engine room. Should a fire break out in the galley or even the head, for example, propulsion, communication, plumbing, and electrical systems will probably remain functional. You'll continue to have a number of resources with which to fight the fire, unless of course the fire gets totally out of control.

Not so if the engine room bursts into flames. A fire in the engine room can completely disable a vessel and all of her systems in a matter of minutes. Electrical systems may melt away. Radio communication may no longer be possible. Engines, fuel pipes, and manifolds, once part of a quite friendly propulsion installation, can turn into dangerous foes.

Fire in other parts of a motorboat is a serious matter, too. Say an omelet gets a little out of hand in the galley. You should have an extinguisher or extinguishers mounted nearby to combat it; remember to always direct the spray at the base of the flames. The strategic location of numerous fire extinguishers throughout your boat is a big part of motorboating safety.

But since engine-room fires aboard boats are the most serious and by far the most common, let's take an in-depth look at how they are best handled.

On most commercial vessels, there's a set of emergency shutdown switches on the bridge, usually marked in red and protected from accidental deployment. These switches make it easy for the watch-standing officer to deal with an engine-room fire in the proper way. He simply flicks the switches in succession.

The tags over the switches are easy to read and reflect certain common-sense procedures that pertain to *any* engine-room fire, whether it be aboard a large commercial vessel or a small recreational motorboat.

There are six critical steps for handling engine-room fires.

1) The first thing to do, even if you only *suspect* an engine-room fire, is shut down the engines. This sounds like great advice, but many people, when under duress, fail to follow it. Why? To most motorboatmen, a functioning engine is the most important part of the boat. In an emergency, even if it be a fire below decks, there's often some hesitancy about shutting down the engines. The fear—and it's of course quite justified—is that if an engine is shut down, it will subsequently refuse to start up again due to the effects of the fire. And once an engine is dead, how will the operator maneuver his boat? How will he ever get home again?

It's easy to understand why motorboatmen think like this. Nevertheless, it's a line of reasoning that can lead to catastrophe. Engines, as well as the rest of the machinery in the engine room, are continually sucking fresh air (fuel for the fire) into the engine room. If allowed to continue to run, this equipment will work to expel any chemical fire-fighting agents present.

So, again, once it's determined, or even suspected, that there's a fire in the engine room, the first thing you should do is shut down *all* machinery. And then, if possible, shut down the fuel supply to any of that machinery. This includes the engines (even if you need them for maneuvering) and generators. Electrical components, such as blowers and fans, should be shut down, too. *Note:* If the engine-room hatches are closed, do not open them, as air will feed the fire.

2) The next step in fighting a fire in the engine room is to close off any access ports or openings where oxygen can enter. Again, the idea is to starve the fire by cutting off its air supply.

3) Trip the Halon or CO_2 (carbon dioxide) smothering system in the machinery spaces if they've not already gone off automatically. Fortunately, many engine rooms today are protected by automatic fire-fighting equipment, such as Halon 1301, a safer extinguishing agent than CO_2, which is unbreathable. And remember, just about the worst thing you can do when you suspect that a fire's been extinguished by one of these fire-fighting agents is to open a hatch to assure yourself that this is indeed the case. More often than not, air will rush in, the fire-fighting agent will be at least partially displaced, and a reflash will occur.

4) The next step in fighting a fire in the engine room is to make a distress call on your VHF. Use channel 16, the international hailing and distress frequency. THIS CALL IS VERY IMPORTANT. With fires of unknown intensity and origin licking away at the engine room, there's no way of knowing exactly how much longer your radio will function. So let somebody know you're in trouble as soon as possible.

Give the name of your vessel, the nature of the distress, and your position. Although you will be tempted to rush, don't hang the mike up until you're

Automatic Halon systems are replacing fire extinguishers filled with oxygen-displacing CO_2 in engine rooms and elsewhere aboard modern motorboats.

confident that the person on the other end is well apprised of your situation and location.

5) Once you're sure the fire is out, don't be in a hurry to check. Open the engine hatches slowly or, better yet, observe the interior of the engine room through a heat-resistant viewing port, if your vessel is equipped with one.

6) Keep in mind that some engine rooms are equipped with automatic CO_2 systems, although the use of this unbreathable gas is steadily becoming more unfashionable. After a fire, any space flooded with CO_2 should be thoroughly aired out before anyone attempts to enter it. Otherwise, asphyxiation may result.

No matter how much fun boating is, it is potentially risky unless you understand and practice the "Rules of the Road." Combine a solid grasp of the rules with commonsense measures, such as reducing speed in crowded waters, and boating can be both exciting and safe.

A SIMPLIFIED VERSION OF THE RULES OF THE ROAD

Because there are no traffic lights, stop signs, or highways on the water, boat operators must observe certain if somewhat abstract conventions when maneuvering around other boats. This way, misunderstandings and the accidents that accompany them are much less likely to occur. It is the responsibility of every motorboatman to become conversant with these conventions. Driving a boat without a decent understanding of what are called the "Rules of the Road" is tantamount to driving a car with no understanding of, or regard for, traffic signals and speed limits.

The Rules of the Road play such an important part in the safe operation of vessels in both inland waters and upon the high seas that all commercial deck officer's licensing exams begin with a set of questions designed to test an applicant's knowledge of them. Much study is called for to pass. If you do not get 90 percent of the questions right, you not only flunk the rules, but you will not be allowed to take the remainder of the test.

Having gone through some sort of licensing exam and a lengthy preparation for it, most commercial people have a pretty good idea of what the rules are and how to interpret them. If, as a recreational motorboatman, you think you've got a beef with some tugboater or bargeman, just remember that to the commercial seaman, the Rules of the Road are tools, things he works with daily to make his living. He probably knows them better than you do.

Recreational boatmen seem to take the rules much less seriously than their commercial friends. Hang around the water long enough and you'll hear all sorts of crazed, self-serving interpretations, like a sportfisherman or the ski-boat jockey who rationalizes his attempt to run a ferryboat out of a channel by claiming, rather vociferously, that commercial traffic is bound to make way for smaller, recreational craft. Or how about the sailboater who maintains that he has the right of way no matter what? The latter argument, of course, is quite as fatuous as the former.

There are several good books dealing with the Rules of the Road. The best I know of is called *Navigation Rules, International-Inland,* published by the United States Coast Guard. It contains both U.S. Inland and International Rules,

which are fairly similar. A more comprehensive and quite lengthy volume is called *Farwell's Rules of the Nautical Road,* and includes commentary.

Given the literature already available, there's no sense trying to explain the rules in their entirety. But we're going to cover the bare essentials, the points you really need to know and follow in order to operate your motorboat safely.

TONNAGE PREVAILS

First of all, when in doubt, tonnage prevails. This is probably the most important and commonsense rule you'll ever come across, although it is *not* contained in the compendium of directions known as the Rules of the Road.

It's quite true that in some instances this rule may disagree totally with the Rules themselves. Nevertheless, I have abided by it to advantage upon many occasions. It's stood the test of time.

Here's a brief example of how it works. I used to regularly travel a hellacious little juncture in the shipping lanes south of Galveston, Texas, called "Malfunction Junction." Malfunction Junction was about one hundred miles (160 km)

Driving a boat without understanding the "Rules of the Road" is comparable to driving a car with no understanding of, or regard for, traffic signals and speed limits.

© Allan Weitz

south of the Galveston sea buoy and it sometimes seemed as though every ship in the world was passing through the area at the same time, altering course, spreading out in every direction, heading for or returning from various ports on the Gulf Coast. On a bad night, the screen of my trusty Decca radar sometimes looked as if it had been hit with a shotgun blast, there were that many ships showing up on it.

In order to get through the area safely on my way to the big semi-submersible oil rigs further south, I'd often just slow down and wait for an opening. Sometimes I'd wait quite a while. It didn't matter whether I had the right of way or not. These ships were big, and manned by people who often had a rather feeble grasp of the English language. They were nice on the radio. They agreed to almost anything I'd suggest. But who knew what they might really do?

Countless are the times that I looked out at a miasma of running lights and range lights, most of them belonging to tankers over eight hundred feet (240 m) long, and said to myself calmly, "Tonnage prevails."

So keep cool. The next time you get into a dicey traffic situation involving a supertanker or a 150-foot (45-m) tug pulling a barge with a few million dollars' worth of wheat, don't get pushy, even if you do have the right of way. You don't want to wind up buried prematurely under the epitaph: "Here lies Old Joe Bright....He's dead now, but he sure was right."

COMMON COURTESY

Motorboatmen should try to give working vessels as wide a berth as possible while sharing the same waterways with them. The commercial man makes his living from the water. Give him a break. Most motorboatmen would be surprised at how much havoc their proximity to larger vessels can create, and how much risk that proximity may involve, both for themselves and others.

One summer Sunday I was wheeling a Great Lakes ore carrier, the *Roger Blough,* up Lake Huron. With another successful run through the Saint Clair River now under my belt, I was feeling quite proud of my developing skills as a helmsman and looking forward to some well-earned relaxation once the captain had vacated the wheelhouse and Walt, the mate, had put the ship on autopilot for the long run up to the Straits of Mackinaw.

Then a crazy sailboat skipper wandered into my afternoon and, in no time at all, utterly destroyed any hopes for the leisurely completion of my watch.

Not long after I first caught sight of this loony bird standing in the cockpit of his boat with the tiller between his legs, he apparently had a brilliant idea. He decided to head straight for the bow of the *Blough,* with the intention of getting very close, I guess, so his starry-eyed crew members could get a good look at what an 858-foot (257.4-m) ship was all about.

Take it from an old ex-tugboatman: Commercial boats really appreciate a little courtesy.

Don't crowd other vessels when passing by them. There's plenty of room on the world's waterways for sailboats and powerboats alike. Remember: in most cases, a sailboat with its mechanical propulsion system switched off has the right of way over a motorboat.

Just prior to the appearance of the skipper and his little red ketch, Walt had rather inconveniently gone below for a moment, leaving the captain of the *Blough* and myself alone on the bridge. The "Old Man," as we called him, was sitting in a long-legged chair over by the radar, with his feet on the windowsill, utterly engrossed in the Detroit paper.

I was engrossed in what the sailboat was doing, but was hesitant to speak in the presence of the captain. Showing a youthful lack of good sense, I began to snake a little wheel on, just a couple of degrees to the right, in order to avoid what I suspected was a collision in the making.

Noticing the course change immediately, but never saying a word, the captain rattled his paper and cast a jaundiced eye at the rudder-angle indicator over the front window. Then he looked at me accusingly, glanced at the sailboat, shook his head, and went back to the comics.

I snuck the few degrees back off. How did the Old Man stay so inhumanly abreast of events? But more important, what were this sailboater's intentions? Suicide?

I started to fidget. Then I cleared my throat. Already, my heart was thumping like a set of war drums. Now it began to pound so hard I thought it might beat a hole in my chest.

"Cap?" I said at last, hoarsely balanced over a chasm of panic. "Do you see that there sailboat coming at us?"

Without taking his nose from the paper, the Old Man, who could read with one eye and watch the lake and its goings-on with the other, replied long-sufferingly, "One of them damn weekend warriors."

He followed this observation up quite stoically with the danger signal (five short blasts of the ship's whistle, repeated over and over again), touched off automatically via a switch on the console.

Then, amid the din, he returned to his chair from the console, picked up his paper again with the air of a man who's done everything that could be done to avoid a fracas, and launched into a powerful and quite colorful tirade of profanity concerning recreational boating in general, which I have deleted here for decency's sake. Then he added, with a tinge of mockery, "Steady as she goes, Pike. To hell with that there sailboat coming at us."

The *Blough* had the right of way, of course. The captain knew the Rules of the Road like Moses knew the Ten Commandments, and he was equally serious about them. We were going to maintain course and speed.

By now the wheelhouse was full of spectators. The danger signal is a big attention-getter aboard ship. A couple of callous souls were actually making bets. Would this nitwit ketch skipper actually sail into the bow of the ship?

It's impossible to describe how it really feels to stand at the helm of a vessel longer than several city blocks, with both hands on the wheel and the danger signal blowing full blast in your ears, watching a little red ketch, with four or five people aboard, some of them children, disappear behind the immensity of a two-story bow.

As luck would have it, the ketch miraculously reappeared, to the tune of a suitably dramatic group gasp in the *Blough*'s wheelhouse, then she ran down our starboard side, the skipper waving and grinning, pointing things out like a proud parent at a Little League baseball game.

"Idiot," fumed the Old Man, as the inordinately lucky fool and his family slid on past. "Idiot...idiot...idiot."

Hopefully, this story makes two points. One, no matter how reliable you think the motors in your motorboat are, trying to get close to a big, commercial vessel for the fun of it is dangerous and irresponsible. Despite the facts that the *Blough* was blowing the danger signal and her watchman was making every sort of gesticulation known to man, the skipper of the sailboat passed ahead of the ship by less than fifty feet (15 m). Had the little boat suddenly lost power or even some of her speed—she was propelled by diesel alone at the time—her skipper and crew would most likely have been killed. Ships are not friendly giants. In shipping channels, big commercial vessels can't stop or maneuver to avoid collisions with smaller vessels. By virtue of size alone, they're physically incapable of it.

Second, sailboats do not always have the right of way. This should be good news to motorboatmen. A sailboat has the same responsibilities as a motorboat when under power, which means propelled by any sort of machinery, whether the sails are hoisted or not.

CROSSING SITUATIONS

Crossing situations can produce accidents if either one or both of the parties involved do not know how they should handle the situation according to the Rules of the Road. A crossing situation is deemed to exist when another boat is holding a course that will cross your own boat's bow from the right or the left. In fact, any boat crossing your bow within an arc measured from dead ahead back to 112.5 degrees on either side is considered a crossing vessel.

If a vessel is approaching from head on, this is a meeting situation. Anything else is an overtaking situation. We'll discuss the latter two situations in a moment.

The easiest way to remember what to do in a crossing situation is to use this memory device. It works best at night, when you can see the other boat's red or green running lights, but it will also work during the day if you bear in mind that all boats have red running lights on the portside and green running lights on the starboard.

Think of a traffic light. When a vessel is crossing from your right, you will see her portside running light, red. You do not actually have to stop, of course. You do, however, have to slow down or alter course so that you pass behind her, or

Hold course and speed.

Slow down on maneuver to pass behind.

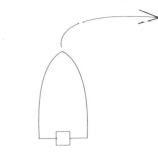

A classic crossing situation. Remember, if you see a green side light on the other boat, maintain course and speed. If you see a red side light, pass astern.

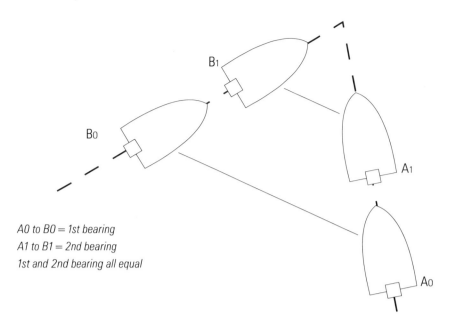

A0 to B0 = 1st bearing
A1 to B1 = 2nd bearing
1st and 2nd bearing all equal

Right: A crossing situation. If the distance between your boat and another lessens while your bearings remain the same, you're in trouble. Below: A meeting situation. Keep to starboard, and you'll be fine.

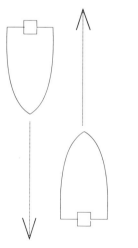

under her stern. When it is obvious that you will pass way ahead of a vessel crossing from your right, you simply continue on without altering course.

When a vessel is crossing from your left, you will see her starboard running light, green. Again, think of a traffic light. Just keep going. Maintain course and speed.

Green for go, red for stop. In a crossing situation, you either hold your course or turn right.

RISK OF COLLISION

There is a way of determining if, in a crossing situation, a risk of a collision exists. Let's say you're cruising along in your motorboat and you see, out there on the horizon, another boat that apparently intends to cross your bow. She's got the right of way. Fine.

But you're not sure whether the other boat's going to be able to cross your bow safely. Maybe, given her current course and speed, and your current course and speed, she's going to hit you. Maybe you've altered course to starboard but aren't quite sure whether it was enough. So you want to know, for your own piece of mind, whether a risk of collision exists.

Here's how to find out. Take a bearing on the other boat. Let some time go by—a few minutes—and then take another. How do you figure the bearing? Experience on the water will eventually give you an eye for it. When I first started running boats in the Gulf of Mexico, I sometimes did not have the foggiest sense of what the boats around me were doing. The sea, even on a bright sunny day, can be a confusing and mysterious place, particularly if you are surrounded by what seems to be a million other boats, all going every which way.

Until you develop an eye for bearings and how they may or may not be changing, use your boat to help you. Find something on the console that is right on the line of sight between your eyes and the vessel you are wondering about. Sight once, then after two or three minutes sight again, making sure that your head is in about the same place as it was the first time.

If the other vessel is still riding your sight line, and the bearing between your vessel and the other boat does not change over a period of several minutes and you draw noticeably closer together, you better alter course radically or radio the skipper of the other boat pronto, or else your whole day is about to be ruined.

There are much more scientific ways of taking bearings. They're not as quick, but they are more accurate. The electronic bearing line (EBL) on a radar works well, for example. So does a pelorus, bearing board, or azimuth circle.

MEETING SITUATION

In a nutshell, when meeting another vessel head on, stay to the right. The preferred method of meeting and passing at sea is portside to portside.

Do not make a fetish out of sticking to the right-hand side of the channel, however. If the most logical method of meeting and passing is starboard to starboard, do not go through a bunch of navigational acrobatics in order to pass in the preferred way.

And remember: If you alter course in any way when meeting another vessel, make the alteration significant enough so that it is readily noticed by the skipper of the other boat. That way, he knows what your intentions are.

OVERTAKING SITUATION

This is the simplest rule of all. If your boat is overtaking another, coming up on it from behind, stay out of the lead vessel's way. The boat that is being overtaken is bound to maintain course and speed.

USING THE RADIO

If there is the least bit of concern over what any other boat's intention actually is, use your VHF radio. There is nothing wrong with identifying your vessel, then calling the other, identifying it by color or location in relation to some familiar landmark, and asking which side the captain wants or whether he is planning to cross your bow or go under your stern.

A PROPER LOOKOUT

Let's end our discussion with one important suggestion. If you keep it in mind, as well as the other rules and suggestions I've already mentioned, you're going to be running a tight, safe ship.

Maintain course and speed.

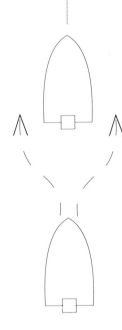

An overtaking situation. The lead vessel has to agree before you make your move.

Maintain a proper lookout. As I've mentioned before, the water can be a deceptive place, especially when you are alone. Most people who spend a lot of time on the water eventually see things they wonder if they really ever saw. Have you ever momentarily mistaken sea gulls sitting on the water at short range for far-off ships and nearly had heart failure in the process? If you spend enough time on motorboats, believe me, you'll eventually see even crazier things, particularly if you add fatigue to the mix. Being tired produces a kind of confusion in which reaction time slows down and relatively familiar stretches of channel begin to look very unfamiliar.

What I am getting at is this: The Rules of the Road emphatically state that boats should have proper lookouts. The rules also state what a proper lookout is: someone who has no other duty but to watch for possible danger.

Technically, any single-handed skipper is breaking the law. He or she cannot be considered a proper lookout because he or she has other responsibilities, such as steering and navigating.

My suggestion is that aboard any motorboat on a long trip, at least two people should be on the bridge, one the driver, the other the lookout. The water world is a much less confusing and scary place when you have got somebody else to filter your impressions through.

SAFETY EQUIPMENT

In chapter 5, we talked about outfitting your boat. While radios, anchors, compasses, depth-sounders, and lorans are very important to the smooth, safe operation of a motorboat, they are surely not more important than the safety gear we are now going to discuss.

Any good motorboat is going to have plenty of accessible stowage room for all required safety equipment.

© Allan Weitz

Should you decide to take a Power Squadron or other boating course, your instructor will no doubt emphasize that safety equipment—or more accurately, basic, well-made safety equipment—is crucial.

Many new boats are now sold with safety gear. If you buy such a boat, check the included gear carefully. Don't take the manufacturer's word that all the gear is there and in proper working order. If something's missing, buy what you need.

Be at least as picky about the safety equipment that often comes as part of a used-boat purchase. If some of the gear is bad, as it may well be, replace it right away. There's no room on a well-found motorboat for ripped and rotting life jackets, damp or outdated flares, or an Emergency Position Indicating Radio Beacon (EPIRB) with a dead battery.

THE PERSONAL FLOTATION DEVICE (PFD)

Everyone aboard a motorboat should have at least one approved PFD. They don't necessarily have to be wearing them, but they've got to have them close at hand.

Life preservers, the old-fashioned term for PFD, may be any of three types: type I, type II, or type III. There are a couple of other types that aren't commonly thought of as PFDs, but we won't bother with them here.

Type I is the bulky kind of PFD, and probably the most recognizable. It is uncomfortable to wear and looks about as fashionable as ear muffs on a dog. It is, however, the best PFD to have on board. The advantage of type I is that it tends to turn an unconscious person in the water from a facedown position into a faceup position so that he can breathe. This type has more buoyancy than the other types.

Type II is more comfortable to wear because it is less bulky. It is also more stylish. It tends to turn an unconscious person faceup, but it does have less buoyancy than type I.

Type III is just as buoyant as type II, but it will not turn an unconscious person faceup. Its fashionable good looks hardly compensate for its inability to keep a person's mouth above the water in a rough sea.

You can equip your boat with any of the three types. The only advantages of types II and III are comfort and the fact that they make you look like a boat advertisement when you put them on. They are the fashion industry's answer to survival at sea.

Fortunately, I have never been cast like bread upon the waters, with only a PFD between me and eternity. But I have been sufficiently close to such a situation to know, for sure, that neither one's appearance nor comfort means much during emergencies. A person in the water is interested in fundamentals, such as a PFD's buoyancy and whether its collar is high enough to support his head.

Type I

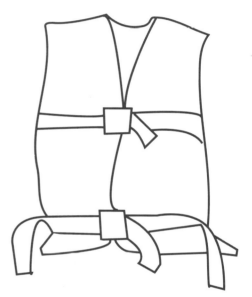

Type II

Type III

SIGNALING METHODS AND DEVICES

A friend of a friend of mine was recently complaining about the callous behavior of the boating crowd on Long Island Sound. The guy said he had some engine problems and was trying to flag somebody down, his portable radio being on the blink.

As you know by now, my friend's friend should have had a regular VHF aboard to begin with. Not a hand-held. My suspicion is that the batteries in his minuscule portable were run down. But all this is neither here nor there.

The distressed boatman was trying to signal his fellows by waving and yelling. The uniform and understandable response to these gestures was a similar wave and a similar yell, all very good-natured, of course. Not only did our stricken boatman not know enough to have a good radio on board, he did not know how to signal properly for help, a skill you can acquire quickly and for which you need absolutely no equipment.

A small-craft boatman in distress can signal others in the following way during daylight hours. Stand at the highest possible and/or most visible location on board the boat. Then stretch your arms out to the side and, repeatedly and fairly slowly, raise and lower them. If this signal doesn't work, you're probably doomed, unless you want to try another daytime signaling method. Hang some kind of incongruous object in the rigging of the boat, such as a boat cushion or a pair of pants. I suppose a pair of garishly colored bloomers would prove to be even more effective, your chance of getting rescued depending entirely upon the amount of embarrassment you were willing to embrace.

For serious (life-threatening) emergencies, the most widely recognized distress signal is the word MAYDAY. It has become much more popular among the distressed since the proliferation of efficient and inexpensive VHF radios. Here is the MAYDAY procedure.

Make sure your VHF is turned to channel 16 (the international hailing and distress frequency), key the mike, and repeat the word MAYDAY three times, following it up with "This is" and the call letters and name of your boat. Then give the following information in this order:

- The nature of your distress
- Your latitude and longitude or bearing and range from a prominent landmark
- The number of persons aboard
- A brief description of your boat (length, color, and any other distinguishing characteristics)

(A friend of mine and his dog were out cruising around one Sunday afternoon when they heard a MAYDAY call on the VHF. In short order, the United States Coast Guard responded. It seems the distressee was actually only aground somewhere, and after switching from channel 16 to another, less crucial frequency to talk, the responding Guardsmen asked the fellow what his position was. "I am the chief loan officer of the First Atlantic Bank," the man replied seriously. "Although I fail to see what that has to do with my present situation.")

Flare guns are usually very dependable devices. The flares, however, are not. Flares have expiration dates, which should be clearly printed on them. Always check to make sure your flares have not expired; if they have, immediately buy new ones, as worn-out flares may fizzle. Why take the chance?

There are other distress signals. One of the most universal is the SOS in Morse code, which is three dots, three dashes, followed by another three dots. Do not get this confused with three dashes, three dots, followed by another three dashes, which does not mean a thing, as far as I know. Morse, of course, can be sent visually or audibly by flashing a light, by horn, even by mirror.

Smokes and flares are popular and useful signaling devices. Some companies sell kits that contain a number of pyrotechnic devices. Just remember, use common sense when dealing with flares. There is no use firing off an orange smoke flare if there is no potential rescuer within a two- to three-mile (3.2- to 4.8-m) visibility range. There is no use firing off a hand flare if there is no obvious help within about five miles (8 m). In desolate areas, a parachute flare should be the first choice. Always try to keep one smoke or flare in reserve for the rescuer's final run in.

EPIRBs

When deployed, Emergency Position Indicating Radio Beacons (EPIRBs) transmit signals that can be picked up either by aircraft in the area, governmental rescue agencies, nearby boats, or, via satellite, other ground-based rescuers. Any motorboat that travels offshore, beyond the range of its VHF, should be equipped with a class-A or class-B EPIRB, although it is not bound by law to do so.

EPIRBs work. In most cases, no less than twenty-four hours will elapse between the time an emergency signal is first received and a full-scale search-and-rescue effort has gotten underway. If this sounds like a long time to you, think about the alternative.

There are three classes of EPIRBs. Class-A types are usually bracket-mounted to a vessel's exterior. They float free if the vessel sinks, and activate automatically. Many commercial boats are required by law to carry class-A-type EPIRBS, which are quite expensive, and may cost several hundred dollars.

From the financial point of view, class-B EPIRBS make a lot more sense for recreational boats. Being cheaper, class-Bs don't include built-in flotation, so buyers often equip them with separate flotation collars. Class-Bs can be activated either manually or automatically.

Both class-A and class-B EPIRBs transmit a distinctive signal on two aircraft frequencies. The signal alerts passing aircraft as far away as two hundred miles (320 km). Satellites, which are monitored by several nations of the world, also receive the signals.

Class-C EPIRBs operate on different frequencies and are intended for use in coastal or inland areas by boats that don't have their own VHF radios. They're the most inexpensive type of EPIRB, often costing less than two hundred dollars. Buying one makes sense if you already have a class-B on board. When deployed, a class-C transmits an emergency signal that is received on VHF channel 16.

courtesy Alden Electric

You'll never miss an EPIRB until you really *need one.*

The "mini-B" is a small EPIRB that can be attached to a personal flotation device, along with reflective patches, a whistle, and a battery-powered light. It would be nice if every personal flotation device could have all these features, including the mini-B.

Recently, another type of EPIRB has been developed, which signals satellites exclusively. Called the Type 406, it transmits a serial number specifically identifying the vessel by means of a descriptive card mailed in at the time of purchase. There are several advantages to this type.

First, inadvertent use of units (false alarms) is better weeded out. This pleases government rescue agencies, which have neither the money nor the time to chase wild geese. Moreover, satellites will no longer have to be in range of a ground station to transmit emergency information; they can store information and pass it on later, when overflying a station's location. The only disadvantage of the new EPIRBs is their cost, which may amount to something like a few thousand dollars per unit. They are too expensive at this point in time to be seriously considered for use on most recreational watercraft.

FUEL AND GAS VAPOR DETECTORS

The thirty-foot (9-m) cabin cruiser was almost brand new. It had a generator installed in its machinery spaces to provide electricity away from the dock for equipment in the head and the galley, and for the lights aboard.

The owners of the boat, a middle-aged man and his wife, had left port for a weekend outing on Saturday morning per usual. Friends became concerned when the couple did not return on Sunday afternoon, as scheduled. A search began.

Eventually, the boat was found anchored in a small cove. Its two occupants, the middle-aged man and his wife, were dead from carbon monoxide poisoning. Apparently, they had left a small generator, which they had improperly installed, running overnight, while they slept.

Although the hazards of carbon monoxide, especially aboard gasoline-powered boats, have been understood for years, carbon monoxide detectors are still not included as standard equipment on many new boats sold today. Certainly, there was no carbon monoxide detector aboard the thirty-footer (9 m) just mentioned, but there should have been.

A properly installed carbon monoxide detector should be part of the safety equipment aboard any modern motorboat. If the manufacturer of your boat did not install one, buy one and install it, or have it installed by someone who knows how.

And while you're at it, make sure your boat is equipped with a gas-vapor detector, an instrument which sniffs your bilges for gasoline, propane, or hydrogen fumes. If there's no gas-vapor detector aboard, buy one and install it. But don't rely on it implicitly. Gas-vapor detectors can malfunction, as can carbon monoxide detectors. Use common sense: It's not a good idea to run a

Aboard a boat, a medical kit is a lot like a sharp pocketknife: not having one when you need one is a real problem. Medical kits can be large and complex, or small and concentrated; either way, they should contain essentials such as bandages, Band-Aids, disinfectant, scissors, and tape.

generator all night, and never crank an engine when your own nose tells you it might be dangerous.

FIRST-AID KITS

No matter what its size, no motorboat should be without a first-aid kit, even if the kit is rudimentary. The rule of thumb here is that the farther from land you venture, the larger your medical kit should be. If you plan to make a long journey, I'd say a course in cardio-pulmonary resuscitation (CPR) and first aid would be in order.

At the least, any motorboat should carry a standard first-aid pack, handily located, with standard dressings, scissors, antiseptic creams, anti-seasickness tablets, and analgesic tablets. This kit should also contain a booklet on first aid, preferably printed on some sort of waterproof paper.

There are any number of kits available, with prices commensurate with complexity. A recent introduction is a dental emergency kit. This is something I wish I'd had along on a stormy trip to Haiti a few years ago, when I lost a tooth to a large socket wrench that hit me in the mouth during a long bout with a towing cable. (To this very day, I remain depressed about the state Haitian dentistry's let itself get into.) The kit contains pre-mixed temporary filling material for use in recementing crowns and bridges or replacing lost fillings. An instruction manual on most common emergencies is included. Somehow, I doubt this approach to home-grown dentistry is going to cause a rash of do-it-yourself dentistry in marinas across the land.

LIFE RAFTS AND LIFE RAFT ETIQUETTE

Let's say the worst happens. You've lost your big displacement motorboat. It's just sunk like a plugged nickel in the middle of the Indian Ocean. What now?

Any offshore motorboat should be outfitted with an inflatable life raft. Because of the way inflatable life rafts are now constructed, they're your best bet for survival, a lot safer than old-fashioned lifeboats.

Life rafts come in several types and sizes and vary primarily in their approach to ballast (weight in the bottom of the boat that maintains balance). The more expensive types employ ballasting material that encircles the bottom of the raft. Other models rely on smaller ballast pockets, which simply hold water.

This ballasting feature is important. When a life raft overturns, its occupants are forced to return to the water and subject themselves again to the risk of drowning and the possible effects of hypothermia, probably the two most serious threats to their safety.

Most life rafts these days are contained in rigid containers, which occupy very little stowage space on deck. They can be activated manually, by simply pulling on a long, well-marked lanyard (or rope) once the canister has been tossed over the side. But most life rafts will activate automatically. After the stricken vessel has sunk below the water, to a depth of about six feet (1.8 m), the raft will deploy itself by means of a hydrostatic release, a device that sets the raft free from its cradle when subjected to a certain head of water pressure.

Once the raft has been released hydrostatically from its lashings, it floats to the surface. The lanyard, the end of which is secured to the vessel, becomes taut and causes the raft to inflate. Eventually the lanyard breaks because of the so-called weak link that attaches it to the vessel. The raft is then set free.

The best life rafts have a double floor and a double tent or canopy to retain body heat and provide an insulating barrier against the elements. Never store a life raft below decks in a valise where you can't get at it in an emergency, and have it inspected once a year by a service technician.

One last piece of advice about life rafts: Fortunately, the chances of the average motorboatman ever actually having to make use of one are slim. But in the event of catastrophe, you're going to have to adapt to circumstances in a hurry. Here's what to expect:

1) Seasickness. Aboard a life raft, even veteran boatmen who are not prone to *mal de mer* will have to contend with its symptoms. The life raft, after all, is enclosed and in constant motion. An abandon-ship bag, whether a commercial or homemade unit, should contain medication to combat seasickness. If you are going to be sick, try desperately to poke your head out of the opening in the canopy, in deference to your colleagues.

2) Democracy in action. Some people are under the impression that there are laws ordaining that the legal commander of the stricken vessel must automatically become the commander of the survival craft at sea. This is not true. In fact, it may not even make very much sense. Maybe the captain is a real half-wit. Maybe you're now floating listlessly around the high seas because he goofed royally.

Unless the captain of the sunken vessel is the obvious leader, by virtue of his experience and stellar qualities of character, a vote should be taken, or some other fairly simple means be employed, to establish leadership. Once a leader has been chosen, allow him to handle distribution of food and water.

3) Depression. Survivors in a small group probably have a better chance than the solitary survivor. They can help each other, keep each other's spirits up, and there's a good chance there will be at least one dominant individual in the group who will resolve to stay alive and help others to do the same. There are numerous tragic tales of people who have succumbed, when one more day would have seen them safely rescued.

4) Possible indecision. Never abandon ship until you're absolutely certain that your boat is going to sink. You're much safer crying peacefully to yourself aboard a half-submerged sportfisherman than you are crying peacefully to yourself in a life raft. Of course, sometimes it's hard to tell exactly when you should give up the ship. How do you know when it's time to go?

Would that all days on the water were as lovely as the one shown here. Ah well. Into each motorboating life, a little rain must fall.

Michael Greenwald, in his book *Survivor,* suggests a method he calls "The Buttocks Rule." It's very simple: When water begins to nuzzle the lower reaches of your buttocks, you can reasonably assume that the vessel is headed for the bottom. Greenwald adds, commonsensically, that the rule must be modified somewhat for very large and very small vessels.

WEATHER TIPS

The whole idea behind understanding the weather and being able to predict it is to make boating safer and more enjoyable. Boating will put you into a much closer relationship with the weather, whether you want to be or not, so you might as well try to understand the elements as best you can.

For the majority of boatmen, the VHF radio is probably the handiest tool of all for understanding the weather. In any given area, there are going to be from two to four weather stations available, broadcasting recorded messages twenty-four hours a day. The messages include general weather conditions, the weather pattern for the next few days, tide data if applicable, and any warnings concerning weather.

Weather forecasts are often quite general, however, and may not apply to a specific area you're interested in. If such is the case, you're going to have to rely on your own skills of observation. We don't have time to get into a full treatment of clouds, their shapes, and what they mean. There are plenty of books around that do this very well.

We do have time, however, for a couple of very general rules of thumb that will keep you out of trouble. Just looking at the sky is often a good indication of what the weather might be up to.

- A grey sky in the early morning usually means fair weather in the afternoon.
- A dull red sky at sunrise or sunset and a lavender sky in the early morning or late afternoon usually presage good weather. A red sky in the morning means the weather is very likely to turn foul before the end of the day.
- If the sky has a golden or brilliant look to it, expect wind. But probably not rain. If the sky has a dull yellow quality, you can count on rain within the next twelve to twenty-four hours.
- Other storm indicators: a sunset with bright white clouds; a sun that looks washed out and weak; a moon with a corona around it.

As for the clouds themselves? Not only does the type of cloud mean something, but so does the pattern or sequence in which it appears. For example, during your weather observations, note whether clouds are increasing or decreasing with the passage of time. Also note whether the clouds seem to be lowering or lifting. In general, thickening and lowering clouds mean rain. Lifting and breaking up of clouds means fair weather's on the way.

Squalls—fast, powerful, and localized storms—are dangerous for those afloat. Often you can detect the approach of a squall line, with its attendant thunderstorms, well in advance by observing at a considerable distance the anvil tops of the cumulonimbus (dense, vertically developed) clouds associated with the line. Because of atmospheric conditions that precede a squall, often only the tops of the anvils will be visible. The bottoms will be hidden by what appears to be hazy blue air. If your boat is equipped with radar, you can often track storms, especially squalls, and predict an encounter almost to the minute.

courtesy U.S. Marine

Sun is always fun, but a good captain always keeps a "weather eye" peeled. Weather can change very quickly on the water.

MORE ADVICE ON SAFETY, OF THE HOME-GROWN VARIETY

Here are two ideas that may come in handy in an emergency. I can't remember who passed the first of these along, but the trick surfaced on a job down in Trinidad some years ago, when a very expensive and very large boat sank in three hundred (90 m) feet of water shortly after her crew abandoned her.

What happened was this. While maneuvering around a drilling rig, the boat struck a sizable piece of steel protruding underneath the water. A hole, less than a foot (30 cm) in diameter, was punched in the engine room. The crew panicked and left the boat without closing any watertight doors or shutting down the engines. The boat sank in a matter of minutes. No one was hurt, but the entire crew was subsequently fired.

Upon hearing of the incident, someone remarked to me that the day could have been saved very easily by employing a couple of common plastic garbage bags. The bags are stuffed inside one another and then stuffed with a couple of pillows and tied-off in the regular way. Then, from outside the hull, the plastic-wrapped wad of pillows is lowered into the vicinity of the hole, where suction seats it. Water pressure holds the plug in place until less temporary repairs can be effected.

Whether this trick actually works or not, I don't know. I've never had a chance to try it out and, God willing, never will. I include it here because, who knows, it might help some motorboatman out someday.

The second idea is the result of bitter experience. Some years ago, I was enjoying a ride aboard a sportfishing boat that base-priced for well over a half million dollars. The boat contained many bilge pumps.

On our way back to the dock, running across Barnegat Bay, a narrow inlet of the Atlantic Ocean extending for thirty miles (48 km) between the eastern coast of New Jersey and a line of offshore islands, we began taking on water due to a glitch in rudder design. When we first noticed the water, it was up to the oil pans of our twin diesels. Electrical wiring for the bilge pumps had already shorted and the pumps were zonked.

The only way we made it back to the dock that day was by using a couple of five-gallon (19-l) buckets and all the energy we could muster. The lesson? Despite the complexity and grandeur of your vessel, bring along a bucket. On big boats, five-gallon (19-l) buckets work fine. On smaller boats, use smaller one- or two-gallon (3.8- or 7.6-l) buckets.

The humble bucket. A very low-tech item to wind up a discussion about safety, especially when you consider the advanced state of technological development most modern motorboats represent. But during a lifetime around boats, I can't think of a single well-outfitted, thoroughly safe vessel, no matter how complex it might have been, that did not have a few simple buckets on board.

Although life rafts aren't standard issue on most motorboats, large models should carry them. Smaller models not built to withstand offshore rigors must be emergency-equipped as well— with life jackets, signaling devices, a good VHF, and a complete first-aid kit.

ALL THE FUN YOU CAN HAVE

© Allan Weitz

So far, we've taken a look at the history of motorboating, the types of boats and engines that are on the market today, and the equipment you should have aboard. Hopefully, this information will help you enjoy boating more and be safer while doing it.

Now let's take a look at some of the fun you can have with motorboats. As we know, people have been motorboating, one way or another, for thousands of years, braving all sorts of weather conditions, eating awful food, undergoing privation and seasickness, all in the name of fun. Because of advances in technology and technique, the modern motorboatman is in a better position to enjoy the sport than ever were his ancestors.

If you already own a boat, I hope the stories and reminiscences that follow will help you remember some of your own good times on the water, even encourage you to take your boat out next weekend, even if you have something else planned.

If you don't own a boat, I hope the next few pages will convince you to get one. I hope you'll begin to appreciate, even if only a little bit, the incredible variety of experiences modern motorboats can offer the sportsman. I hope you'll start to see that maybe, just maybe, you too were born to be a motorboatman, and that you should join the rest of us, as we follow our bliss.

There's just something about motorboats…a mystique compounded of speed, faraway places, and being at home on the water.

REBUILDING OLD BOATS

I bought my first used boat in Salem, Massachusetts. I borrowed money from a friend to come up with the purchase price. The boat was a twenty-two-footer (6.6 m) and the guy that sold it to me was a lucky man. The boat was a veritable wreck. As I proudly hauled it away from the boat yard on a dilapidated trailer, a local sage was heard to say, "There goes another one, born again."

The next year was spent deeply involved, on weekends and on some nights after work, rebuilding that boat. My goal was to turn a robin's-egg blue catastrophe into a kelly green-and-buff-colored masterpiece. For a long time, it seemed as though all of my efforts were absolutely futile. But eventually, the old boat began to look like a new boat.

Rebuilding an old boat is an exhausting, sometimes depressing, but ultimately rewarding thing to do. Don't let anyone kid you: It is not a cheap endeavor.

Of course, when I bought that first boat, the idea that I was paying so little was one of the selling points. As the restoration began, the glow of my presumed savings obscured, or sometimes obscured, the fact that I was now spending quite a lot of money on paint, electrical components, and engine parts. About halfway through the project, the truth began to dawn on me, but I was hooked on the boat by then. In the end, though, I undoubtedly saved myself quite a bundle of money by buying an old boat and fixing it up. But the bundle was considerably smaller than I had anticipated initially.

Since that first boat, I've rebuilt others, some wooden, some fiberglass, some a combination of the two building materials. Based on these experiences, I can safely say that, at least for me, fixing up an old boat can be a source of great pleasure. I would certainly recommend it for spendthrifts and skinflints alike.

For me, the planning of a restoration provides infinite pleasure and entertainment. I've spent many nights in the bunk of a tugboat, hundreds of miles from the nearest marine discount store, dreaming of some boat ashore and how I would fix her up. My cabin strewn with catalogs and books, I've lain awake for hours on end, anticipating, seeing with my mind's eye the transformation of some beaten-up hulk into a thing of beauty, a work of art.

There are literally thousands of old boats lying around to choose from these days. Most of them are made of fiberglass; seemingly eternal, many of the original boats built in this medium twenty-five years ago are still around and basically sound. You can often buy these boats for less than a couple of thousand dollars. Replace or refurbish the brightwork, patch and paint the hull with Awlgrip, Imron, or some other good paint, and sooner than later you're the owner of what appears to be a brand-new boat.

Old wooden boats, however, are much fewer in number. This drawback is offset by the fact that usually the old woodies can be had for a good deal less money than old fiberglass boats. And old wooden boats aren't really that hard to restore, unless the candidate for restoration is very old and very complicated.

Rebuilding an old mahogany runabout is a challenging job, one that requires a level of skill that cannot be developed overnight. If you're not an utter purist, however, you can save yourself some study and sweat by buying a replica or having one built. In most cases, only you will know the difference.

For a newcomer to the field of wooden-boat restoration, it would be advantageous to apprentice with a builder for a while or study the subject at a boat-building school. But such things are hardly necessary to assure success. In terms of knowledge, I rebuilt my first wooden boat from scratch, not knowing a knee (a triangular-shaped structural member) from a carline (a fore-and-aft structural member). Besides what the experience itself taught me as I went along, magazines and books were my only other source of instruction. The mistakes I made helped me learn a lot, too.

Restoring old boats, as opposed to buying new ones, has more than monetary advantages. A year's worth of spare time spent rebuilding an old boat will teach you more about boating than several years of buying and trading off new ones. But don't spend all your time rebuilding and restoring; you'll miss all the fun that's to be had on the water.

During my days at the maritime academy, I took a course on ship construction, the bulk of which was devoted to terminology. Somehow, none of this terminology really stuck with me until I began to relate it to the boats I'd rebuilt in the past. Construction terminology is much the same, whether you're talking large ships or small wooden boats.

Old fiberglass boats may fade away somewhat, but they never die. This means that, right now, there are an awful lot of candidates for restoration hiding in backyards and boat yard junk piles.

If you decide to rebuild an old boat, you can take comfort in the knowledge that there is a whole slew of modern products on the shelves of marine stores that will make your job easier. You can buy everything from goop-on leak stoppers to hand-moldable epoxy, workable putty that sticks to fiberglass, metal, glass, and wood, even ceramic surfaces. In emergency situations, a waterproof epoxy putty can be applied above or below the waterline of a boat and will cure in approximately twenty minutes. If your candidate for resurrection is a fiberglass boat, you're probably going to run across a miracle drug for old boats sooner or later: epoxy resin. Epoxy resin is good for all types of problems. Whether your boat's got loose hardware, holes and punctures, gel coat blistering, transom delamination, delamination of coring materials, or cracks, crazing, and scratches, you'll find that epoxy resin and associated products will come in very handy.

Some of the best material on the market is W.E.S.T. System epoxy (Gougeon Brothers, Inc., 100 Patterson Avenue, P.O. Box X908, Bay City, Michigan, USA 48707), with which you can effect repairs that may often be stronger than the original structure. Gougeon Brothers even sells a repair-and-maintenance manual and a videotape that takes you, step by step, from basic mixing and handling procedures to making fillets, rebuilding cored panels (without access to the back of the repair area), bonding hardware, and fixing gel-coat blisters.

Epoxy can be quite helpful in the restoration of wooden boats, too. So can other products from such companies as BoatLife, Interlux, and Petit. Often, by using materials that are more commonly associated with fiberglass construction, you can improve upon a wooden boat's strength and its looks.

Restore an old boat, and you've got an instant conversation piece.

© Allan Weitz

© Neil Rabinowitz

One of the most important prerequisites for the proper rejuvenation of an old motorboat is finding a place to work that is clean and well lighted. Trying to work with today's high-tech glues and resins, fillers and paints, while fighting the weather or even variable temperatures is one of the best ways I know of to contract ulcers. What money you do save by buying a used boat, you'll lose in medical bills.

Don't be surprised when a restoration project occasionally feels more like a penance than a joy. A little gloom and doom lavished on a pocket of unexpected dry rot will pay off in the end by adding extra piquancy to the launch. I'll never forget the day I launched the twenty-two-footer (6.6 m). You can own a house, I believe, and never have a full sense of ownership. With a motorboat, this is quite impossible, especially if you've taken the time to rebuild it.

Rebuild an old boat and you'll own it in much the same way a pioneer owns the land he or she has cleared. Feelings of pride and ownership are enhanced when the boat floats, of course, leaks only modestly, and plows off through the waves just as she was meant to, once the motor's started.

SPEED ON THE WATER

There are two important facts you should know about the modern speedboat: One, it costs more money, per displacement pound, than any other type of boat. A veteran race driver told me several years ago that, above about sixty miles (96 km) per hour, a buyer should expect to pay almost $10,000 for each extra mile per hour added to the top hamper. The price has probably gone up since then. Two, going fast in a motorboat on the water bears little resemblance to going fast on the highway.

Any truly adventurous soul, anyone who's truly interested in motorboats and all the things they can do, should go fast on the water, at least once. And not sort of fast, either, but really fast.

The fastest I've had the good fortune to go is 115 miles (184 km) per hour. I was in the company of an experienced race driver, Stuart Hayim. Despite a bit of a wild streak, he's a calm man with a calm voice, the mellifluous sound of which can be very soothing when you're idling in the swells with the bow poised on an empty horizon and two Lightning Performance engines growling like evil spirits at an exorcist. To pass the time while not competing in offshore powerboat races, Stuart sells carpets and rugs on a grand scale. His Skater catamaran, built by Douglas Marine Corporation, Douglas, Michigan, when

Why are human beings so attracted to going fast? Speedboats give operators a sense of mastery, escape, and freedom that is difficult to duplicate with any other means of transport.

fully rigged and powered with a set of Lightnings capable of a combined horsepower of about 1,680, retails for about $250,000.

We ran the boat on a smooth September Sunday afternoon. It was a clear, Indian-summer day. Stuart let me drive. Exactly why, I'm not sure. Perhaps it has something to do with the fact that Stuart's a recovering cancer patient; he races boats to prove to other people that cancer can be beaten, that an active life can be lived in spite of disease. The man is a walking, talking definition of healthy optimism, which means there's probably some fatalism mixed into his Weltanschauung.

During my 115-mile (184-km) -per-hour driving lesson, we hit a four-foot (1.2-m) wave thrown up by the combined effects of several wakes. The catamaran literally flew through the air, Lord knows how far, and frankly scared the living daylights out of me. As a group, racing catamarans are probably the fastest boats on earth. But they have a downside. They tend to "blow-over." Sometimes, a fatal trick.

Once we'd touched down with a resounding whomp and Stuart had throttled down to a comfortable seventy-five miles (120 km) per hour so we could talk, I was constrained to remark, rather nervously, that offshore race boating is not for the faint of heart, nor is it for the inexperienced.

Speedboats can be elegant, no question about it. Drop into a cushy driver's seat, sit behind a custom steering wheel, and go tooling down a palm-fringed canal. It's guaranteed to boost your morale.

HOW TO DRIVE 100 MILES (160 KM) PER HOUR

Driving a boat faster than eighty miles (128 km) per hour takes so much concentration I'd be lying if I said it was fun. It's work. Do it only in the company of a professional or some other knowledgeable person.

At high speeds, a boat handles nothing like a car. It rises so far out of the water that it handles more like an airplane. And because its drives, tabs, rudders, and other control surfaces are skimming the water at such high speeds, the driver must exert control with exquisite subtlety. Professionals know that any major movements of the wheel, or major adjustments to trim, can get them into trouble.

Drivers also know they may be called upon to use some muscle, too. Sometimes steering an offshore boat in rough seas is tougher than trying to steer an eighteen-wheeler down a twisted dirt road with the power steering on the blink.

Serious speed is serious business. At speeds in excess of eighty miles (128 km) per hour, any driver, no matter how good he is, will be so busy steering that he will have no time to think of guests in the backseat. The best bet is to leave passengers ashore if you're thinking of really tearing up the lake.

While driving a fast boat, you should watch the water far ahead. If you're watching the area just forward of the bow, you are looking at the past.

Should the boat leave the water, as it often will when running offshore in heavy sea conditions, the throttles must be pulled back momentarily, or else the engines will overspeed and cause damage to the transmissions, drives, running gear, or the engines themselves.

Most professional speedboat drivers will tell you that high-performance driving is a two-person job. One person steers, and the other monitors engine gauges, operates the throttles, and controls the attitude of the boat via drive and trim-tab adjustments.

A good throttle man can make an inexperienced driver look good. He will seldom cut power to stabilize a situation. He knows that adding more power ensures control. Take the power off a fast boat and it will fall on its face. A good throttle man pulls the throttles back as little as possible, with a rhythm that fits the wave pattern the boat is riding.

HIGH-PERFORMANCE BOATS

Speed on the water is not entirely the purview of race boats. As mentioned in chapter 2, there are any number of off-the-rack high-performance boats that can take you to the very edge. You can buy these boats or cultivate friends who own them.

Prior to my experience with the Skater Cat, about the fastest boat I'd ever driven was an outboard-powered bass boat that was capable of doing about

Some commercially available boats are capable of speeds in excess of 130 miles (208 km) per hour. It takes years of experience and nerves of steel to drive a boat safely at such speeds. If you're inexperienced, drive a speedboat only in the company of a seasoned driver.

© Allan Weitz

eighty miles (128 km) per hour. Bass boats have a very low profile; they're basically flat fishing platforms, with one or more pedestal seats. Driving that bass boat across Lake Macatawa, in Michigan, was like piloting a flying barn door.

The most immense or ponderous sensation of speed I've ever felt came aboard an eighty-odd-foot (24-odd-m), $5.25 million Monterey sportfisherman, *Renegade,* in the Atlantic Ocean off the coast of Fort Lauderdale, Florida. The boat weighed a little over sixty tons (54 metric t) and topped out at around fifty-five miles (88 km) per hour.

Actually, sixty tons is light for a vessel of this size. Construction of lightweight, high-tech coring materials, such as Divinycell, balsa, and Nomex, kept the weight down. Even the furniture was cored. What appeared to be solid hardwood chairs, tables, and beds were really constructs of Nomex (an air-filled paper product) and expensive, very thin veneers. You could hoist a whole king-sized hardwood bed over your head with one hand.

The engines on this monster? From the land of the Nibelung: twin MTU 16V 396 TB94s with 3,460 shaft horsepower each, fully computerized, electrically controlled, and monitored.

Riding on this baby was fun, of course, especially while standing on the flying bridge at top speed. To get a better idea of the feeling, imagine what it would be like to climb onto the roof of a good-sized tract house and ride it over some six-to eight-foot (9.8- to 24-m) seas at close to fifty-five miles (88 km) per hour.

Safety first. At megaspeed, professional drivers wear special helmets and impact jackets. Their boats are equipped with kill switches and, to decrease the level of distraction, an extra crew member, a throttleman who controls the engines and monitors instrumentation.

The sensation of going fast on water is like no other. It's more like flying an airplane than driving a car ...at tree-top level or less.

A FEW WORDS ON GAS GUZZLING AND SAFETY

Speed is not for everyone. In fact, speed isn't really for me. As was pointed out in the beginning of this book, I'm a trawler-type guy, most comfortable with speeds in the neighborhood of seven to fourteen knots.

The world of motorboating is fast filling up with trawler types like myself. Displacement hulls and efficient diesel engines are the new wave. Eventually, the era of gas-guzzling speed demons that roar around the nation's waterways, frightening dogs, small children, and me, will end. In many ways, that's too bad; there's nothing like a modern high-performance speedboat.

Someday, people who burn one hundred gallons (380 l) of gasoline per hour, or two hundred gallons (760 l) of diesel fuel per hour, whether in high-performance boats, motoryachts, or sportfishermen, will be considered irresponsible. Burning outrageous amounts of fuel is a stupid thing to do. One wonders why boat builders, like automobile manufacturers, aren't trying to find ways to build boats that are more efficient and cheaper to run.

But listen, all you red-blooded motorboaters. Before the gas crunch finally crunches, before the twilight years of the Great Guzzle fade, take advantage of the fast-boat frenzy. It's the last hurrah. Get a fast boat, or at least a ride in one.

Sure, the feeling of mastery that speed on the water can give you is pure illusion. But so is a good movie. And upon the surface of the earth, speed on the water is the last frontier.

Where high speed is concerned, safety on the water is crucial. The most fundamental drawback about having an accident on the water is that you can't walk away from it, as you sometimes can from an automobile accident on land. Victims of accidents on land are almost always immediately accessible to rescue crews.

Not so, victims of accidents on the water. The water, for all the fun it can offer the motorboatman, is an alien environment. Wear a personal flotation device. If you're going to indulge yourself in a fast ride in an open boat, wear a helmet, an impact jacket, and a "kill switch" lanyard (a cord, one end of which is fastened to an engine cutoff switch, the other end being attached to the driver).

Impact jackets protect the chest in a crash. They also have high, Count Dracula–like collars and unequal amounts of flotation material, front and back. In the event of an accident, an impact jacket will roll an unconscious person over onto his back and keep his head elevated above the surface of the water. Wearing a helmet makes sense, of course, because it protects the head. And the kill switch shuts down the engines of the boat should the driver be thrown clear in an accident.

Another thing to keep in mind when driving fast is that under optimum conditions, some boats, like the Skater Cat in relatively flat water, or a mono-hull Cigarette or Aronow in a light chop, handle so sweetly that they lull you into a feeling of false security. Cockpits are so well designed and so high tech that they insulate you from the evidence of extremely rapid transit.

© Christopher Bain

courtesy OMC

Will the end of the gas-guzzling years bring with it a return to oars? No, but you can expect cleaner, more fuel-efficient engine technology and an entirely new era of motorboating.

Driving or riding in a very fast boat, under optimum conditions, can be such a pleasant and exhilarating experience that you forget how fast you're really going and how rapidly traffic and other situations are changing. The only reminder is the amazing rapidity with which objects, like other boats, buoys, or floating debris, approach.

This advice certainly bears repeating: Do not try to plumb the secrets of speed without a competent guide. Learn how to drive fast by driving slow first. Increase your top speed in easy increments, so you never feel uncomfortable or scared. Remember that the Rules of the Road apply, no matter how fast you are going.

Most high-performance boat companies provide some instruction to new owners. Some even include videotapes on driving with the purchase of each new boat.

FISHING... FROM MEXICO TO MATOON CREEK

My most recent fishing trip took place in Mexico, near Isla Mujeres (the Island of Women), which floats free of the coast, in the warm green fringes of the indigo ink of the Yucatán Channel. My wife and I spent about a week living in a motel on the island, fishing for swordfish during the day on a boat that belongs to a friend of mine. It was mid-April, typical early-season weather. Clear and cool, offshore.

Actually, I think I'm sort of idealizing the whole trip in retrospect, as I'm wont to do sometimes. On the first day of fishing, we took our boat, a sixty-three-foot (19-m) ocean sportfisherman, about a hundred miles (160 km) offshore. When we began trolling, running back and forth in the troughs between the seas, my wife got sick. Not mildly ill. Sick as a dog.

She held off begging to return to land until I'd caught and released one fifty-odd-pounder (22.5 kg). The captain of the boat was determined not to return. A hundred miles (160 km) is a long way to go for just one fish. But I eventually, if halfheartedly, convinced him we should go back.

In the days that followed, I fished without my wife. It was an enjoyable time, but tinged with guilt. Was my wife okay back there among strangers? But I deserved to feel uneasy. I'd taken a person to sea on a fishing trip without the slightest idea of whether she was really prone to seasickness or not. That's a no-no.

While I worried, my wife had a heck of a time. She spent her days sight-seeing, trying out incredibly cheap but good restaurants, and buying Mayan art.

In the evening, we'd wander through the moonlit streets of the town, which were crammed with pariah dogs and mysterious old women. Then we'd go dancing at the clubs. We liked two in particular because they were frequented by a very entertaining man who dressed like Zorro minus the mask. What a dancer. Never had we seen a person who could abandon himself to such passionate self-dramatization, especially during love songs featuring the words, *Mi corazón*.

So how do you go sportfishing in exotic places? If you don't own a boat or know someone who does, you can find charter vessels of just about every size and description.

But don't fish exclusively. The extracurricular things you do and the shoreside places you see will enhance your big-game fishing immensely. Fishing and fine food ashore complement each other.

Before you invite your friends and family to accompany you on your next fishing trip, make sure they're ... ... (left) do, too.

HERE FISHY, FISHY, FISHY

What's it like to catch a marlin or a sailfish? Or a giant tuna? Trolling for big-game fish, hour after hour, no matter how snazzy the boat, is boring. At least for me. Nothing happens. The sun beats down. You sweat. Diesel fumes waft about. The outriggers seem to scrape the sky. Time drags on. God help you if you've got a hangover. It'd be fine if you could go to sleep, but you can't. You've got to stare into the boat's wake, for hours on end, watching for birds, tide lines, debris, anything that might indicate the presence of fish.

Dazed by the sun, you eventually fall to fantasizing about what it's like to catch a fish, fondly turning over in your mind the flurry of activity that accompanies every strike. On a clear day, sunglasses aren't a luxury or a fashion statement, they're a necessity.

Then somebody yells "strike" and a fish jumps.

A desultory camaraderie that was really commiseration suddenly turns electric, becomes the camaraderie of an overattended athletic event. People are crawling all over themselves and each other, trying to clear the cockpit of gear and lines that might get in the way.

You set the hook with a short, violent flick of the rod tip. Then you bust a gut getting yourself strapped into the fighting chair. The battle has been joined.

There's a very atavistic quality to the struggle. Its physical symptoms are often manifested as chills going up the spine. But chills soon can turn to exhaustion. You pull the rod tip up, then crank the reel. You do it again. You may do it for hours. It's surprising the amount of effort required to land even a sixty-pound (27-kg) sailfish.

Once the fish is brought to the boat, it should be tagged and released. Killing fish has become pretty unfashionable during these days of dwindling resources, at least among the conservation-minded.

If you don't have access to a big sportfisherman or the wherewithal to charter one, welcome to the club. You don't need a big boat to catch big fish. Fighting chairs are regularly mounted on small, center-console fishing boats to good advantage.

Here's a true story. A fellow from Hawaii caught a giant tuna from an inflatable dinghy. Because he suspected that no one would believe his story, he brought the fish back to port, towing the varmint in a boat half its size.

Fishing for small fish from small boats can be just as rewarding as fishing for large fish in large boats. Inland fishing is particularly enjoyable if your boat is trailerable. Once you get the hang of it, trailering a boat can take you to all sorts of places, sometimes very distant ones. It can provide you and your family with entertainment and adventure.

Small-boat fishing can be a meditative kind of endeavor, even if there are four people and a dog crammed into your twenty-six-footer (7.8 m). Small-boat

The character of big game fishing is no longer the same. Today's anglers release their catches. For trophy hunters bent on having something to hang on their walls, modern taxidermists can create fiberglass-and-plastic replicas using photographs taken prior to release.

© Darrell Jones

fishing can be exciting, too. You can't beat the wild feeling you get from the gentle deadliness of a fly rod, for example, with multiple back casts snaking over your shoulder, as graceful as a dance. And how many hearts have been lifted up by the sound of a spin caster's fast flick, followed by a long, mechanical whir as the line and lure reach out like a benediction over the smooth green surface of the water.

When I was a boy, I used to go fishing in a plywood runabout on a creek that flowed behind my house. My father went with me once. We went up near the railroad trestle, where hemlock trees grew on one bank and cows grazed on the other. There was an old pink pumphouse among the hemlocks, and once in a while the pump would go on, piping the bark-colored water over the hill to the ponds of the golf course beyond the woods.

The night was moonlit, the sky was the sort of blue that can't be duplicated outside of nature. Somehow, after you fish long enough—and unsuccessfully enough—in a little boat, you get closer to people. My father told me some things about himself that night about how he tried to live his life that I don't think I'd have ever heard otherwise.

Ask any one of these three guys if fishing in small boats isn't at least as much fun as fishing in big ones.

THE COMPLETE BOOK OF MOTORBOATING

CRUISING

There were three of us aboard: my daughter, my son, and myself. The boat's name was *Readership,* and she was a thirty-two-foot (9.6-m) cabin cruiser built by a company that has a reputation for practicality, quality, and good, solid accommodations. There was a cabin for my daughter at the stern, another on the bow for my son. I slept on a fold-out sofa in the salon in between. While under way, we lived on the flying bridge, amid tubes of suntan lotion, books, charts, and an endless parade of cold sodas from the refrigerator in the galley.

We traveled for a week. It doesn't really matter where. Cruising is not so much a function of place as it is a state of mind.

Our minds were full of late August and the smell of the ocean and the coast. Our days went like this: Everybody woke up when they wanted to. The boat could be undocked single-handedly, so there was no need to wake anybody up to shove off. By midweek, we were all rising around eight o'clock. It just worked out that way. Eight o'clock seems a little late, but since all of us were reading mindless trash half the night, this gave us all about eight hours of sleep. Which is healthy.

THE MORNING

On those mornings we woke up tied to a dock in some quaint harbor town, we'd take showers, get dressed, and then go ashore for breakfast. Meals on land taste even better if you know you're going to be leaving soon for a day on the water.

Sometimes, we'd check out a store or two on the way back to the boat. Innocent of involvement, we'd watch the commercial side of the town come to life. Maybe we'd run a few errands. We'd pick up a tank of cooking gas for the barbecue, which was clamped to the stainless steel rail around the afterdeck, and maybe we'd have to rent three bicycles and ride halfway across an island to get the gas. Maybe we'd buy a plastic blowup shark to float around on during the evening swim fests. Whatever.

Once back on board, we'd start looking over the chart, figuring where we were going to go next, what we were going to do. Eventually, we'd come to a decision.

There is no better feeling in all of motorboating than the one you get just before turning the ignition key at the helm of a cruising boat, when you know she's provisioned to the gunwales, equipped with all the gear you need and should have, and you have an idea of where you're headed for the day, and at the same time, you don't.

If we were low on fuel, we'd go over to the fuel dock, tie up, and fill our two tanks. Then we'd pull away, usually with a wave to the dockhand, and point our bow toward the wild blue yonder.

Today's small cruising motorboat is a veritable home afloat, a sort of nautical cottage

courtesy Grady-White Boats

LUNCH

The most economical speed to run most cruising boats is about two-thirds throttle, which is where I would keep our throttles set en route to the next destination. My daughter would lie on the lounge at the back of the flying bridge and read. My son and I would sit at the helm and shoot the breeze.

Our talks were usually very uncomplicated. We'd talk about the weather. What we'd hear on the VHF. Whether we liked the looks of a passing boat or not. What we ought to have for lunch. Why sea gulls look so clean but pigeons don't.

Around noon or so, we'd have some sandwiches. Maybe we'd stop the boat and drift if the conditions were right. It's surprising how hot it feels once you stop moving on a warm summer day, with the nearest shade tree twenty miles (32 km) away.

After lunch, we'd run a few more hours, then stop for the night. One of the best places we stayed was a lagoon, tough to get into and isolated, with a sand bottom and clear, cool water.

SUPPER

Once inside, the lagoon was protected from wind and seas on every side. It was a quiet place. During two days at anchor there, we went swimming each evening, while our supper was cooked jointly by the grill on the afterdeck and the alcohol stove in the galley. Supper was simple fare: canned corn, boiled potatoes, a salad, and a hamburger with catsup.

By the time supper was over, it was usually close to sundown. The sense of immediacy, of connectedness with the natural world that is found aboard boats at times like this obliterates the concerns we have when ashore. What is important is being together, warm inside our own little floating house, with an immensity of white stars and blue-black sky darkening the companionway.

GOOD NIGHT

Then we'd read a book for a few hours or bundle up in a sweater and watch the night from a lawn chair on the back deck, listening to the water lap the hull, watching the sheen on the lagoon change as clouds cross the moon. Then we'd go to bed.

Of course, wherever you choose to cruise, it's never quite as idyllic as I've described. Don't let me kid you. Brothers and sisters sometimes don't get along. Even with their father. A wonderful friend ashore can turn out to be hell's own houseguest afloat. Weather can turn bad and stay that way.

But for the most part, over a lifetime that has included a lot of different cruises, the ritual seems to be pretty much the same. If you want to cruise, just do it. It's a modern world, but idylls surround us still. Almost everywhere.

ALL THE FUN YOU CAN HAVE

BOAT ANATOMY

1. **FLYING BRIDGE**
2. **COCKPIT**
3. **GUNWALE**
4. **HATCH**
5. **FOREDECK**
6. **CHINES**

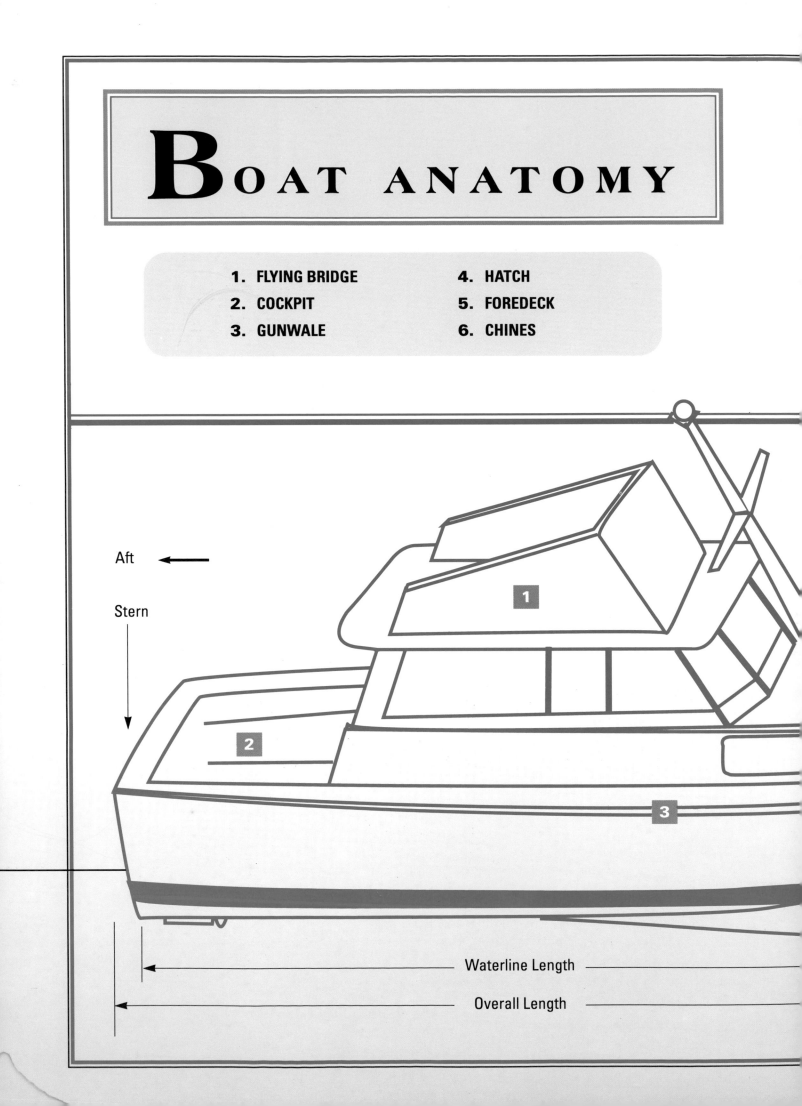

Aft

Stern

Waterline Length

Overall Length

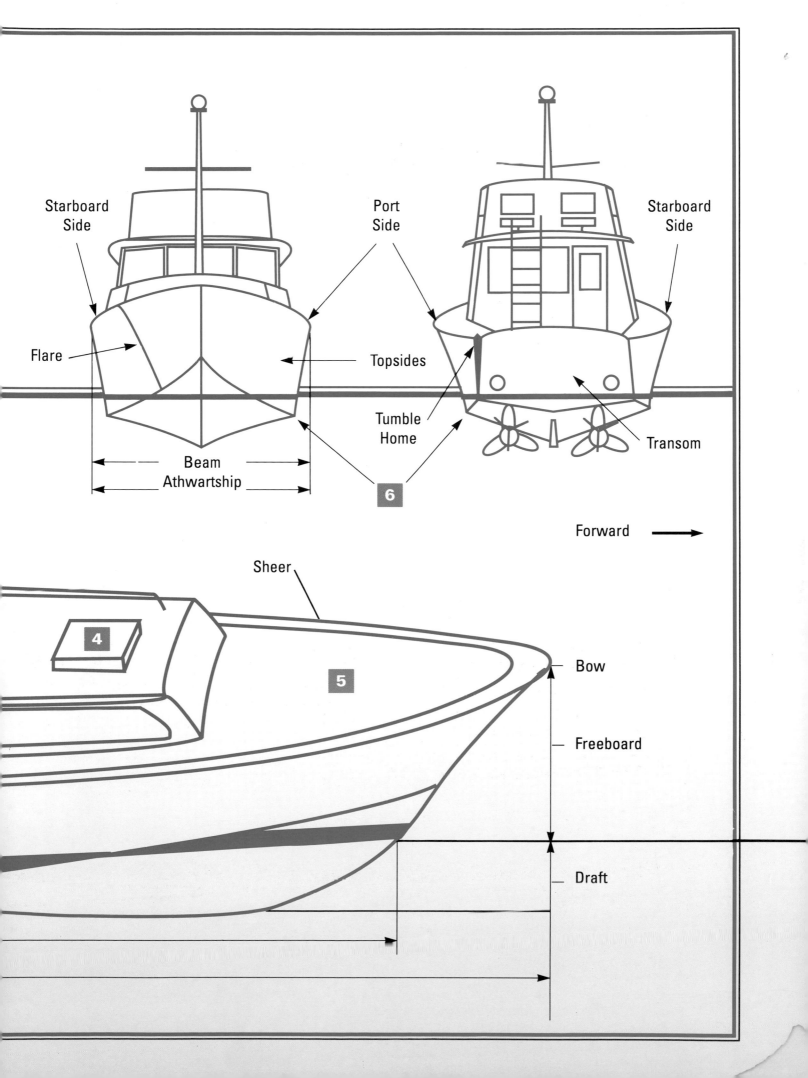

Starboard
Side

Port
Side

Starboard
Side

Flare

Topsides

Tumble
Home

Transom

Beam
Athwartship

6

Forward

Sheer

4

5

Bow

Freeboard

Draft

BIBLIOGRAPHY

Armstrong, Bob. *Getting Started in Powerboating.* Camden, ME: International Marine Publishing Company, 1990.

Barrett, J. Lee. *Speed Boat Kings.* Berrien Springs, MI: Hardscrabble Books, 1986.

Beardow, Keith. *The Volvo Penta Aquamatic Boat Engine.* North Pomfret, VT: David & Charles, Inc., 1980

Beebe, Robert P. *Voyaging under Power.* New York: Seven Seas Press, 1975.

Bowditch, Nathaniel. *American Practical Navigator.* 2 vols. Washington, D.C.: Defense Mapping Agency Hydrographic Center, 1977.

Calder, Nigel. *Marine Diesel Engines.* Camden, ME: International Marine Publishing, 1987.

Chapman, Charles F. *Chapman Piloting.* New York: Hearst Marine Books, 1989.

Farwell, Raymond F. *Farwell's Rules of the Nautical Road.* Annapolis, MD: Naval Institute Press, 1977.

Ferguson, Barbara, and Don Ferguson. *Fishing to Win!* Ft. Lauderdale, FL: Diamond Advertising & Publishing Company, 1988.

Fostle, D.W. *Speedboat.* Mystic, CT: Mystic Seaport Museum Stores and United States Historical Society, 1988.

Franzoni, Roberto. *Riva.* Milan: Automobilia Mare, 1986.

Greenwald, Michael. *Survivor.* San Diego, CA: Blue Horizons Press, 1989.

_____. *The Cruising Chef Cookbook.* Coral Gables, FL: TAB Books, 1977.

Herd, Shirley. *Seawoman's Handbook.* San Diego, CA: S. Deal & Associates, 1989.

Knight, Austin M. *Knight's Modern Seamanship.* New York: Van Nostrand Reinhold Company, 1977.

Lee, E.C.B., and Kenneth Lee. *Safety and Survival at Sea.* New York: W.W. Norton & Company, Inc., 1971.

Martenhoff, Jim. *The Powerboat Handbook.* New York: Winchester Press, 1975.

McEwen, William A., and Alice H. Lewis. *Encyclopedia of Nautical Knowledge.* Centreville, MD: Cornell Maritime Press, 1985.

Naranjo, Ralph. *Boatyards & Marinas.* Camden, ME: International Marine Publishing Company, 1988.

Reale, Thomas, and Michael Johnson. *Your Boat Belowdecks.* New York: Hearst Marine Books, 1990.

Robinson, Bill. *Cruising the Easy Way.* New York: W.W. Norton & Company, Inc., 1990.

Rodengen, Jeffrey L. *The Legend of Chris-Craft.* Ft. Lauderdale, FL: Write Stuff Syndicate, Inc., 1988.

Scharff, Robert. *Complete Boating Handbook.* New York: McGraw-Hill Book Company, Inc., 1955.

Scharff, Robert. *Esquire's Book of Boating.* New York: Esquire, Inc., 1964.

Speltz, Robert. *The Real Runabouts I.* Lake Mills, IA: Graphic Publishing Company, Inc., 1987.

Stapleton, Sid. *Stapleton's Powerboat Bible.* New York: Hearst Marine Books, 1989.

Street, Donald M. *The Ocean Sailing Yacht.* New York: W.W. Norton & Company, Inc., 1973.

Taggart, Robert. *Marine Propulsion Principles & Evolution.* Houston, TX: Gulf Publishing Company, 1969.

Time-Life Books, eds. *Feats and Wisdom of the Ancients.* Alexandria, VA: The Time Inc. Book Company, 1990.

Webb, W.J. *The Pictorial History of Outboard Motors.* New York: Renaissance Editions, Inc., 1976.

West, Jack. *Boatowner's Guide to Radar.* Camden, ME: International Marine Publishing Company, 1988.

_____. *Modern Powerboats.* New York: Van Nostrand Reinhold Company, 1970.

Willis, Melvin D.C. *Boatbuilding and Repairing with Fiberglass.* Camden, ME: International Marine Publishing Company, 1977

GLOSSARY

Abaft: Toward the back end or stern of a boat.

Abeam: Abreast of a boat's side or at right angles to it.

Aboard: Upon or in a boat.

Acceleration: Rate at which velocity of a motorboat increases per unit of time.

Accommodations: Living areas aboard a boat.

Aft: At, near, or toward the stern of a boat.

Ahead: Lying in front of a boat or in the direction of its course.

Aids to navigation: Buoys, lights, fog signals, or any other charted or published information designed to promote safe navigation.

Almanac, nautical: Publication containing computed positions of celestial bodies in the celestial sphere at regular intervals throughout the year.

Amidships: In the vicinity of a boat's middle.

Anchor: A heavy metal hook that, when lowered to the bottom of the sea on a cable, chain, or rope, keeps a vessel from drifting away.

Anchor chocks: Deck hardware designed to guide and hold anchor rode, usually while the anchor is deployed.

Athwartship: Crosswise in a boat.

Autopilot: A mechanical device used to steer a boat automatically.

Azimuth circle: A circular navigational device that can be turned and aimed to establish the relative bearing of an object.

Ballast: Weight in the bottom of a boat to help make it more stable.

Bank: A number of oars that are operated by rowers seated on one bench.

Beam: The extreme width of a boat.

Bearing: Direction from one object to another object.

Belly: The broadest part of a boat's hull, below the waterline.

Below: Underneath the deck of a boat. The accommodations aboard a boat.

Berth: Bed or bunk on which to rest. A dockside place where a boat is kept.

Bilge: The lowermost part of the interior of a boat.

Bimini: A rectangular-shaped awning held in place by a set of folding metal poles. Usually found on boats under thirty feet (9 m) and used to protect occupants from the elements.

Blister: A small patch of delamination in a fiberglass hull.

Blow-over: When air rushing beneath the hull of a speedboat lifts it too much, causing it to flip over.

Bow: The front portion of a boat.

Bulkhead: An upright partition separating one compartment or cabin from another inside a boat.

Carline: Piece of timber running fore and aft between two deck beams, at the ends of a deck hatch or other opening in a deck.

Catamaran: Any boat with two hulls side by side, joined by a "web," or platform.

Caulk: To force oakum or some other fiber into the seams between the planks covering the exterior of a boat's hull. Done to prevent leaks, usually by means of a specialized tool called a "caulking iron" and a mallet.

Cavitation: A partial vacuum around propeller blades that is caused when propeller shaft speed exceeds the speed at which the propeller attains maximum thrust.

Counter-rotating propellers: A set of otherwise identical propellers on a boat, one of which turns in one direction, say counterclockwise, while the other turns in the opposite direction, clockwise. Propellers produce a handling bias; that is, a single-propeller boat will favor either port or starboard. The use of counter-rotating propellers cancel out this bias. For example, a boat with counter-rotating propellers should back up straight, without pulling to the right or the left.

Course: The direction a boat is traveling, usually given in degrees or in the points of a compass.

Cruiser: A boat that is outfitted in such a way as to make traveling about comfortable. Usually has berths or beds and cooking facilities.

Davy Jones's locker: The bottom of the sea. The place where those who are lost at sea wind up.

Dead ahead: Immediately in front of a vessel.

Depth-sounder: An electronic device that determines the depth of water beneath a boat by sending signals to the bottom and measuring the time it takes for them to return to the surface.

Detente: A notch in the shifting lever of an engine control, so you can feel when the engine is in neutral, ahead, or reverse.

Deviation: Magnetic-compass error caused by a boat's magnetism. Also the angle by which true north and magnetic north vary.

Displacement: The weight of a boat. Also, the weight of fluid displaced by the boat when floating in that fluid.

Draft: The maximum distance a hull extends under the water. Deep-draft refers to a vessel with a lot of its hull underwater.

Drive train: The mechanical parts that convey the rotary motion of an engine to a means of propulsion, like a propeller.

Engine: A machine that changes some natural phenomena, such as heat, into mechanical power and movement. Major engine types include steam reciprocating, steam turbine, internal combustion, and electric motor.

EPIRB (Emergency Position Indicating Radio Beacon): A safety device that, during and after a boating emergency, transmits a signal to rescuers.

Fathometer: See Depth-sounder.

Fine: Long and sharp. For example, a fine bow.

Fix: A calculated position, obtained through the use of a sextant, GPS, loran, satnav, or some other positioning device.

Flam: The degree of flare in a bow.

Flare: The curvature of a bow that tends to knock spray down.

Flopper-stoppers: A set of devices, sometimes called paravanes, deployed on booms or poles, on either side of a displacement boat, that stabilizes it, reducing the amount of roll or sideways motion while underway. Flopper-stoppers are baskets with wire mesh in their bottoms; they have rubber flaps that allow the basket to sink readily, but make it difficult to raise. They are used when the boat is at anchor.

Fluke: The flat or bladelike portion of an anchor that digs into the bottom.

Forward: Toward the front of a boat.

Frame: Any one of many structures inside the "skin" of a wooden boat that constitute the skeleton of the vessel.

Freeboard: The distance from the level of the water to the top edge of the deck amidships.

Gain: A quality found in various electronic instruments and equipment related to the strength of signal.

Galley: The area of a boat designated for cooking. Also, a large boat propelled by oars.

GPS (Global Positioning System): A very sophisticated system of navigation that positions vessels by means of satellites and a receiver carried aboard. When all satellites are up, it will be effective twenty-four hours a day, anywhere in the world.

Gunwale (gunnel): The upper edge of a boat's side.

Gyrocompass: A compass that employs a gyroscope to give it directionality. It is subject to fewer types of error than a magnetic compass.

Hatch: An opening in a deck or bulkhead and the protective device that covers it.

Head: The compartment of a boat that contains the toilet. The toilet itself.

Helm: The device by which a boat is steered. The area of a boat near the steering wheel. Also, the amount the steering wheel is turned by the helmsman, as in "twenty degrees of helm."

Hook: Slang for anchor. "On the hook" means at anchor.

Horsepower: A measure of engine power, equivalent to 550 foot-pounds of work per second.

Hull: That part of a boat that is found below the deck.

Inboard: Within a boat, as opposed to outboard, which means outside a boat.

Kapok: A silky fiber from the seed pods of a tree that grows primarily in West Africa. Used extensively in so-called life preservers.

Keel: A long fin on the centerline of a boat's bottom used to improve steering characteristics and tracking.

Ketch: Two-masted sailing vessel.

Kill switch: A switch on the dashboard of a high-performance boat that, when flicked, shuts down the engines. Usually a lanyard, or cord, is attached to the switch. The opposite end of the cord is clipped to the operator of the boat so that if he or she is thrown out, the engines stop and there's no chance the boat will continue to run and injure people in the water.

Knot: A geographic distance established by the British admiralty as 6,080 feet (1,824 m). One knot equals one statute mile (5,280 feet, or 1,584 m) multiplied by 1.15.

Latitude: Angular distance north or south of the equator, normally expressed in degrees.

Launch: To make a boat slide from the land into the water, usually on some sort of skid or track.

Line: A general term for a length of rope or other cordage.

Locker: A bin or other stowage spot, usually protected by a door or hatch.

Longitude: Angular distance east or west of the prime meridian or the meridian circle that passes through Greenwich, England. Normally measured in degrees.

Loran: A navigational system that positions vessels by means of shore-based stations and a loran receiver carried aboard. Works best for coast-wise navigation.

Loudhailer: A device used to magnify the voice aboard a boat.

Manila: A kind of hemp, from a species of banana tree, native to the Philippines, used to make rope for mooring and other lines.

Mast: A polelike device, made of wood, metal, or fiberglass, at the very top of a vessel. Often used to support radar scanners, radio antennas, etc.

MAYDAY: The spoken word to be used in case of life-threatening emergency. Corresponds to the French pronunciation of "m'aidez."

Megayacht: A very large motoryacht, often as much as eighty feet (24 m) or more in length, with a high level of luxury aboard.

Midship: The middle part of a boat.

Mooring: To anchor a vessel or tie her up to a dock. Also, a very heavy, more or less permanent anchor, with cable, chain, and a float, used instead of a boat's own anchor to hold position in fairly deep water.

Nausea: Seemingly fatal sickness, accompanied by vomiting and a loathing of most food. Also called seasickness.

Nylon: A synthetic fiber that can be woven into rope or line. Is stronger than manila, and is also lighter and easy to handle. It is very elastic.

Oakum: Loose hemp fiber often used to caulk wooden boats.

Outboard: Toward the exterior of a boat or outside of it. Also, a portable motor, which is attached to the transom of a boat to propel it. Usually gasoline powered.

Pad eye: A heavy fitting with a hole in it, usually fitted on a load-dissipating pad to a deck or bulkhead. Often used to secure a line, chain, or piece of equipment.

Pelorus: A simple compass card in the form of a metal plate, fitted with sight vanes for taking bearings on distant objects. Usually found in places where the use of a real compass would be impractical.

Pile or Piling: A timber driven into the bottom of a body of water, usually as part of a dock or pier. Often used to secure or hold a boat in place by means of its mooring lines.

Port: A place where boats and boatmen may find shelter. Also, the left-hand side of a boat when facing ahead.

Powerhead: The top of an outboard motor, where the pistons and flywheel are.

Powerplant: Slang for the engine or engines in a boat.

Print-through: A condition found in some fiberglass boat hulls where the texture of the glass cloth shows through the surface.

Puddle jumper: A very small boat.

Radar: An electronic device that depicts on a CRT (cathode ray tube) screen what the navigator can't see, either because of darkness or weather conditions.

Range: A set of lights or markers, situated fore and aft in a channel, something like a giant rifle sight, used to indicate to boats when they are moving up or down where the center of the channel is located.

Rode: The rope that is attached to the anchor at one end, and to the boat at the other.

Roll: The movement of a vessel from side to side in a seaway.

Rudder: A vertical piece of wood, fiberglass, or metal, usually located at the stern of a boat and mounted on a shaft or "stock" that allows it to turn and thus steer the vessel.

Runabout: A small boat, with a cockpit that can accommodate a driver and several passengers, used to make short day trips.

Running aground: Inadvertently driving a boat into water that is shallower than its draft. Hard aground means that it is very difficult to remove the boat to deeper water.

Running attitude: The angle at which a boat interfaces with the water while under way.

Running gear: The parts of a boat outside the hull that propel and steer it. Most often, the term is applicable to the rudders and propellers of inboard boats.

Satnav: Satellite navigator or device that positions vessels by means of satellites and a satnav receiver carried aboard. Subject to periodic coverage. There are considerable time lapses between readings, which makes satnav unfit for most coastal navigation.

Seaway: The motion of the waves in the ocean.

Sextant: A device that measures the angle between the apparent horizon and a celestial body. This information can be used in conjunction with an accurate measure of time, such as the *Nautical Almanac* and sight-reduction tables, to determine an approximate position at sea.

Skeg: A short fin running along the centerline of a boat's bottom that is used to improve its steering characteristics and tracking.

Ski boat: A small, runabout-type boat built to pull waterskiers, often with an automotive-type engine mounted inside, in the middle of the cockpit.

Slip: A place ashore, usually with walkways on three sides, where a boat is kept.

Sole: The floor of a cockpit or cabin.

Solenoid: An electrical conductor wound with wire so that when an electrical current passes through it, it establishes a magnetic field.

Sounding: A notation on a chart that lets the navigator know what depth of water he or she may expect in a certain area. Also, the physical act of determining the depth of water using some type of physical means.

Sportfisherman: A large big-game fishing boat, usually more than thirty feet (9 m) long. Also, a person who fishes from such a boat.

Stability: The tendency of a boat to return to her original position when inclined therefrom.

Starboard: The right-hand side of a vessel when facing forward.

Stern: The back of a boat.

Stern drive: A propulsion system that puts the engine inside the boat, and an outboard-motorlike drive unit, with a propeller that is aimed in the direction you want to go in the water, abaft, or behind the transom.

Stock: The heavy, central part of an anchor to which the rode is attached.

Stow: To put things aboard a boat.

Stowage: The facilities, in aggregate, where things can be stored aboard a boat.

Stringer: A long, rectangular beamlike structural member in the bottom of a boat used to strengthen its hull.

Surface-piercing drive: A propulsion system in which a propeller or propellers are not immersed in the water but only slightly pierce or touch it.

Tender: A small boat, often less than twelve feet (3.6 m) long, that is used to travel back and forth between the shore and a larger boat at anchor.

Tooling: Shapes, usually made of wood and various shaping compounds, that are used to create the molds for fiberglass boats.

Tracking: A boat's ability to maintain a straight course with minimal adjustment of the wheel.

Transom: The aftermost strengthening surface of a boat's hull. The surface of the boat at the stern.

Trawler: A displacement, or non-planing, cruiser with a high, angular superstructure or cabin. Usually looks like a trawler-type fishing boat.

T-Top: A bimini-like awning with a characteristic T shape, found mostly on center-console fishing boats, to protect occupants from the elements.

Universal joint: A set of U-shaped parts, often found in a drive train that, when connected, allow for flexibility or the introduction of a different direction into the drive train.

Variation: Compass error caused by the discrepancy between the earth's magnetic and geographical north poles.

Vessel: Any watercraft that is used for navigation. Often a large craft, with a continuous deck to protect it from the entrance of seawater.

Wake: Water behind a boat that is disturbed by the vessel's passage.

Waterproof: The ability to entirely keep water out.

Water-resistant: The ability to resist the dampening effects of water.

Waypoint: A theoretical or actual point used in navigation as a goal or intermediate goal.

Wheel: A screw propeller. Or the wheel by which a boat is steered. Also, the act of steering a boat.

Wheelhouse: The cabin aboard a boat where the navigational gear is fitted, such as the wheel, compass, etc.

Windlass: A machine, usually mounted on the bow of a boat, that lifts the anchor from the bottom by means of a motor or engine.